KT-456-118

# contents

# teach® yourself

## winning at
## job interviews
igor s. popovich

2016

Launched in 1938, the **teach yourself** series grew rapidly in response to the world's wartime needs. Loved and trusted by over 50 million readers, the series has continued to respond to society's changing interests and passions and now, 70 years on, includes over 500 titles, from Arabic and Beekeeping to Yoga and Zulu. What would you like to learn?

be where you want to be with **teach yourself**

4712684

For UK order enquiries: please contact Bookpoint Ltd, 130 Milton Park, Abingdon, Oxon, OX14 4SB. Telephone: +44 (0) 1235 827720. Fax: +44 (0) 1235 400454. Lines are open 09.00–17.00, Monday to Saturday, with a 24-hour message answering service. Details about our titles and how to order are available at www.teachyourself.co.uk

Long renowned as the authoritative source for self-guided learning – with more than 50 million copies sold worldwide – the **teach yourself** series includes over 500 titles in the fields of languages, crafts, hobbies, business, computing and education.

*British Library Cataloguing in Publication Data*: a catalogue record for this title is available from the British Library.

ISBN-10: 0 340 85976 8
ISBN-13: 978 0340 859 766

First published in UK 2001 by Hodder Education, part of Hachette Livre UK, 338 Euston Road, London, NW1 3BH.

This edition published 2003.

The **teach yourself** name is a registered trade mark of Hodder Headline.

Copyright © 1994, 2000, 2003 Igor S. Popovich

Typeset by Transet Limited, Coventry, England.
Printed in Great Britain for Hodder Education, an Hachette Livre UK Company, 338 Euston Road, London NW1 3BH, by Cox & Wyman Ltd, Reading, Berkshire.

The publisher has used its best endeavours to ensure that the URLs for external websites referred to in this book are correct and active at the time of going to press. However, the publisher and the author have no responsibility for the websites and can make no guarantee that a site will remain live or that the content will remain relevant, decent or appropriate.

Hachette Livre UK's policy is to use papers that are natural, renewable and recyclable products and made from wood grown in sustainable forests. The logging and manufacturing processes are expected to conform to the environmental regulations of the country of origin.

Impression number 10 9 8 7 6
Year                2010 2009 2008

Contae na Mídhe

## Dedication

To my parents, Slobodan and Ela, for their love and support through all those years of sacrifice.

about the author

Igor S. Popovich was born in Yugoslavia. He started his professional career as a research engineer and university lecturer. In 1988 he migrated to Perth, Australia.

During his considerable professional engineering experience in Europe and Australia, mostly in the mining/mineral processing industry, oil and gas sector and tertiary education, Igor has been managing employees, consultants and contractors on various engineering, management and safety projects.

Igor is the author of five internationally published management books, the latest being *Managing Consultants* and *KAIZEN and YOU – Success Through Constant Improvement*. Igor is the creator and leader of the highly acclaimed internationally presented management seminars *How to Manage Consultants, Negotiation Strategies and Tactics* and *Powerful Presentations*.

As a consultant, Igor helps individual and corporate clients with various aspects of personal and organizational improvement.

Igor's engaging, humorous and enthusiastic style makes him a highly sought-after presenter of management and technical seminars. He is able to present dull, misunderstood and complex topics in a simple, illustrative and enjoyable manner. This ability blends naturally with his gregarious and open personality and enables him to arouse interest and provoke thinking. He knows how to motivate participants and get them actively involved in discussions and practical exercises.

He is currently working on his PhD thesis at the University of Western Australia, researching the area of knowledge management in management consulting.

For more information on Igor's seminars and other books, write to: Igor Popovich, Career Professionals, 14 Fitzgerald Loop, Canning Vale WA 6155, Australia.

## From the same author

*Your Job – How To Get It, How To Keep It,* Simon and
  Schuster, Singapore
*The Complete Australian Job Interview Guide,* Austed Publishing
  Company, Australia
*Managing Consultants,* Century, UK (out of print)
*KAIZEN and YOU – Success Through Constant Improvement,*
  Management 2000, UK

**introduction**

In this chapter you will learn:

- about the skills and strategies needed in successful job-hunting
- about the various professionals who can help you achieve your goals
- about the importance of the job interview and how to get the most out of this book

*The future never just happened. It was created.*

Will and Ariel Durant, *The Lessons of History*

## What they *do* teach you at university

I started my university studies in the early 1980s. I was keen, I studied hard and my grades were excellent. Sometimes it was fun, but it was never easy. Some people found it too difficult, but I was prepared for the five years of hard labour. From the beginning, the signs were there. In the introductory lecture, one of the professors said to more than 450 freshers: 'Today you are entering the Faculty of Electrical Engineering. It is one of the most reputable schools in the country. The degrees obtained here are recognized in most western countries and highly regarded by employers. You will have to master a range of different subjects, you'll have to pass calculus, differential equations, statistics, solid state physics, and other difficult courses. Take my word for it, you'll learn engineering and you'll enjoy it. But don't fool yourselves: it won't be easy to get there. I'll give you an idea off how difficult it is going to be. I want you to take a good look at the person on your left and at the person on your right hand side. Only one of you will become a graduate engineer.'

All of his predictions came true, except one – the electrical engineering programme was dull and hostile to our young minds and I didn't enjoy it. All I enjoyed was the relief after passing the exams. Every time I would feel closer to my ultimate goal. It was almost like our lecturers had a boot camp mentality: 'I went through it, now you've got to go through it.'

I will never forget the day I did the presentation of my thesis and received the official certificate (graduation ceremony took place two months later). I felt like I was on the top of the world. All my dreams came true and all that hard work came into fruition: I became *somebody*! The world was my oyster. I managed to get a job as a research and development engineer and part-time lecturer at the university in my home town. I had plenty of free time to pursue my interests. English was one of them. That's when the idea to move to Australia was born. When I came 'Down under' in 1988, the whole range of new opportunities opened in front of me. But things were not that easy in the beginning. All that glittered wasn't gold!

# What they *don't* teach you at university

It took me about two years to realize how little I knew. Not about electrical engineering, but about the real world. Hundreds of available jobs in the local paper every Saturday lured me into thinking that getting the right one would be a piece of cake. The only problem was that I didn't know how to go about it or where to start. The whole system was new to me: jobs, résumés, interviews, employment agencies, application letters, competition, …

With a little help from my friends, my eyes started to open and soon I mastered the skill for what proved to be the second biggest challenge in my life: the art of getting a job and keeping it. Keeping it was relatively easy, the first part was the tricky one. After more than 200 applications and about 20 interviews I finally landed my first professional job. Since I'm one of the people who constantly seek something better, more challenging and more rewarding, in the following four years I changed jobs four times and moved three times.

Each job was easier to get than the previous ones. I had a good command of the English language, relevant local experience, relatively good references, and, above all, I knew how to sell myself and how to be 'The One' amongst 40 or more engineers who applied for the same job.

Nobody taught me how to do it. I had to learn the hard way – through my own experience. Much later I discovered self-improvement books. They became my best allies and helped me reinforce my knowledge of the job-finding process and various related areas: communicating with people, negotiating, public speaking, selling techniques, technical and business writing, management methods, leadership and many others.

# The importance of neglected skills

It took me more than 25 years to realize a simple truth about the most valuable skills in life: the so-called 'broad' or 'generalist' skills. The most important amongst them is definitely the ability to relate to people and to communicate with them through speech, manners, body language and writing.

Those are the skills that can – and if you posses them will – get you employed and keep you there. The sad truth is that you won't learn how to acquire or improve them in school. The only way to do this is through your own efforts. This book should help you bridge the gap in your education.

Very early in the job-hunting process I developed a habit. After each unsuccessful interview I would sit down and write everything I could remember about it: the questions, the interviewer's style, behaviour and comments, names and facts, figures and impressions. Very slowly, a pattern started to emerge. Some questions were repeated more often than the others and I started to recognize the mistakes I made in each particular case: wrong answers, wrong gestures, inappropriate questions, poor posture.

As I was improving my résumé and my performance at interviews, the recession was spreading at an unprecedented pace and getting the right job was becoming more and more difficult. My newly acquired skills were put more and more to the test each time I applied for a job. That was when the idea of writing this book was born. Unemployment rose above 10% and I felt that was the time to share my experiences with other job hunters, who, like myself, are constantly searching for the 'magic' wand that will get them that elusive job of their dreams.

My book is now in your hands. For the next 200 or so pages I'll lead you through the strange world of employment interviewing. As happens in life, you may not agree with everything I say. That's perfectly normal, I don't expect you to.

The main purpose of this book is to start you thinking about employment interviews and to give you a foundation for using your own ideas, methods and tactics in interviewing.

It was a difficult and tedious task to search the existing literature in the area of interviewing, to read every possible book that even remotely mentioned the word interview, and to compile all relevant information together with my own experience in one compact book that can serve as a universal guide to job seekers from various backgrounds and professions.

## My reasons for writing this book

Being a Libra, I have always highly valued justice, fairness and individual achievements. My engineering degree reinforced my belief in logic and reason. Later I realized that the real world is hardly based on logic. It is based on feelings.

Furthermore, I have always had sympathy for the individuals who never surrender, for the fighters who constantly try to change things for better and challenge the system, particularly if it's wrong.

Combining all those traits, one can hardly be surprised by my desire to help the amateur job seekers who are severely disadvantaged in their dealings with professional players in the job game: recruiters, personnel officers and employment consultants.

On a more general scale, most problems stem from the fact that people deal with 'professionals' in every sphere of their lives. Recruiters, doctors, real-estate agents, lawyers, used car salesmen, bank managers, government clerks, accountants and other professional 'users and abusers' have a distinct advantage over most people, so they can (and do) manipulate us (the unwary amateurs) in the process. The onus is on the users of those services (in this case the job hunters) to educate themselves in various areas and protect their interests.

> *You had better learn how to swim with the sharks, or risk being eaten alive!*

# The purpose of this book

Even after studying this book and applying the knowledge you will acquire at interviews, you will not automatically become an expert in interviewing. However, your chances for success in dealing with employers will skyrocket and give you a distinct advantage over your competitors.

*Teach Yourself Winning at Job Interviews* is my contribution to your education. By reading it, you will make a giant step towards success in job hunting. You may agree or disagree with some of my views and recommendations. Some tactics may work for you, others may not. The final judgement will be yours.

Should you find this book useful in your interviewing, recommend it to your friends who are looking for a job. They will probably be grateful to you for sharing your 'secrets' with them.

Your success will be easy to measure: you will either get a job or you won't. The measure of my success will be the fact that this book has found its way to people who need advice, and has helped them to get the desired job. In that case, I would consider my mission accomplished.

*It is much more difficult to get a job than to keep it.*

# The people who get ahead

The world we live in is not based on logic, justice or equality. These are just the ideals we humans have been trying to achieve for ages. Apart from our efforts, knowledge and hard work, our success depends also on emotions, luck and interaction between people. That's probably one of the reasons why the best, the smartest and the most capable people are not always at the top (there are some exemptions to this rule, fortunately).

*The people who get ahead are not necessarily smarter. They simply have the better understanding of their influence and they are not afraid to exercise it. While their rivals are making a recommendation, the winners are already in action.*

M.H. McCormack, *The 110% Solution*

As a direct consequence, the world is not as good as it could be. Middle class is rapidly disappearing in today's society. In other words: the rich are getting richer and the poor are becoming even poorer.

Let's start by asking a simple question: What could an ordinary person, like you and me, do to stay on the brighter side of the street? Unfortunately, the answer to that question is not simple. Hundreds of books have been written to solve one or more pieces of this puzzle. There are literally thousands of self-improvement books at your disposal, dealing with a vast variety of subjects, all trying to help you achieve your goals, no matter what they are.

*There is only one success in life: To be able to live your life the way you want.*

Christopher Morley

# Strategies for success

I believe that all available facts, tactics and strategies for success could be summarized by the following five points:

- Get as much education and acquire as much knowledge and know-how as possible.
- Find an interesting, well paying job with good career prospects.
- Mix with successful people and use them to go up the corporate and social ladders.
- Invest your hard-earned money wisely and create your 'nest egg' for retirement.
- Retire after accumulating the amount of money that will enable you to 'live comfortably ever after'.

This may sound simple or trivial, but you would be surprised at the number of people who fail to achieve even one of those five goals. The tricky part is that the achievement of each step is usually a prerequisite for the next one. It's like climbing a ladder. The safest and easiest way is not to jump steps, otherwise you may end up like numerous fallen entrepreneurial stars: in court, bankrupt, in jail or all three.

# Getting professional help

On the road to success you'll meet various people who may help you achieve your goals – accountants, financial advisers, bank managers, lawyers and the like. Some of them are honest, hard-working people who can give you the right advice and help you immensely. But beware – as in any trade, there are con artists around. These people can hardly wait to rip you off.

*All professions are conspiracies against the laity.*

George Bernard Shaw

# Finding a job

Now we come back to the second step on the road to success! You have probably asked yourself 'what is so difficult about getting the right job?' It is that most of the time no one can help you to get the job of your dreams. You will have to do it all by yourself. (As for any rule there are some exceptions – if your father is the General Manager or Chief Executive Officer, this might not apply to you!).

But, you'll say, I can get some help from employment agencies, résumé preparation services, friends who can recommend me to their employers, and so on. That's true, but keep in mind that you will have to do most of the work to land a good job. Nobody will bring it to you on a silver plate.

# Doing it yourself

Nobody can make a good career plan for you, nor can anyone attend a job interview in your place. You will be there on your own, so you had better prepare yourself for the challenge.

*There are two times in life when you are totally alone: just before you die and just before you go in for a job interview.*

In this book we will talk about career management. However, due to the complexity of the subject and the fact that all aspects cannot be covered in a single book (if the job is done properly), we will focus our attention on one of the most important steps (if not the most important) in a job-hunting process – the job interview.

I bet the mere thought of a job interview makes your palms sweat and increases your pulse rate. I believe the reason for such reaction is that subconsciously you recognize the importance of the event. Your whole future life may depend upon the outcome of a single job interview, whether you will or will not get that particular job, the one that can enhance your chances of achieving success.

*December is the worst month to look for a job. The other bad months are January, April, June, February, November, July, October, August, March, May and September.*

## Job interviews

You obviously recognize the importance of a job interview, otherwise you would not be reading this book. The rules, principles and examples outlined are based on real-life situations, common sense and a lot of research. The text is easy to follow and you do not need the knowledge of calculus, cash flow analysis, or a PhD in psychology. All you need is honesty with yourself, the desire to improve, keen determination and, as is usual in life, some luck.

You will probably want to know if the tactics and strategies outlined it this book always work. They don't. Nothing does. But they will be the closest you can get to the 'magic wand'.

There is no panacea, no universal recipe that works every time. Every job interview is different and the whole process is influenced by many factors that can make an impact on the final outcome. But by following certain rules and preparing properly you can gain control over most of these obstacles and traps for the unwary.

*Because interviews are so predictable, they are controllable!*

If you prepare yourself for the questions you'll be asked, if you deliver the right answers in the right manner and if you project a positive image of yourself, your chances of getting the job you want will improve dramatically.

There is only a limited number of questions that you can be asked to answer during a job interview. Most interviewers will ask you the same questions because what they want to hear are the same right answers. It is your job to provide the answers they want to hear. That is why the skeleton of your answers will remain unchanged. I have produced these skeletons for you. Don't change them radically. Adjust them to suit your situation and, if necessary, add information to complement them.

Of course the words, accent and tone of voice interviewers will use to ask those questions will vary. These are minor variations and make the job of answering clichéd questions more interesting.

# How to get the most out of this book

You have already made the first and most difficult step towards successful interviewing – you have recognized the need to improve your interviewing skills. Every step that follows will be easier to master if you follow some basic rules. The main point you have to remember is that it is impossible to master any skill by merely reading how to do it. You have to practise – by yourself first, then with a friend or a relative, and finally at real interviews. Each unsuccessful interview will be a lesson to remember. Don't consider it a failure. If you learn just one simple truth per interview, you'll be one step closer towards your goal.

These are my suggestions on how to use this book:

- Read the whole book once or twice, marking those questions in Chapter 6, that could apply to your situation and are hence relevant to you.
- Do a complete and honest evaluation of yourself, your strengths and weaknesses. If you haven't done this already, before writing your résumé, this is your last chance to do it. Identify the critical points and make a plan of action for rectifying or neutralizing the bad ones and emphasizing and reinforcing the good ones.
- Do a thorough search on the particular employer. Use all known facts in the preparation of your answers. This will enable you to show your knowledge of the company and create a positive impression on the interviewer.
- Customize the answers to suit your particular case and the job you will be interviewed for.
- Practise answering the questions. The more time you devote to practice, the more successful you'll be. You can even record the questions and answers and play them over and

over until they 'sit' in your mind, or get a friend or relative to videotape you while answering the questions or to play the role of the interviewer. That would help you evaluate and correct not only your answers and tone of voice, but also your posture, gestures and body language. Don't worry about over-rehearsing. Even if you know the answers 'by heart', there is no danger that you will sound superficial. You will keep changing your tone and pitch of voice naturally, because your subconscious mind will be telling you to do so.

# The question of ethics

If you feel that preparing yourself for the interview, customizing your answers to suit the occasion (which is different from lying) and using appropriate tactics to counteract the ones interviewers use, may not be ethical or fair, think again. If you want to stay poor or unemployed, fine. If not, you'd better adopt some guerrilla tactics.

*The end justifies the means.*
Niccolo Machiavelli

This book will not teach you how to cheat, lie or blatantly falsify your answers. I strongly disagree with such methods and advise you not to use them. Despite what Machiavelli says, there is *no* end that can justify *all* the means.

However, there is a difference between lying and telling the interviewers what they want to hear. In the latter case you simply disclose enough information to improve your chances and avoid unveiling the negatives, which can have a negative impact on the interviewers.

Despite the fact that glibness and prevarication shouldn't be used at a job interview, as much as one-quarter of all applicants can be expected to cheat. According to J.P. McAward, president of the New York investigating agency McAward Associates, 'about 25% of job candidates can be expected to falsify their answers to some application questions. The most misrepresented is the individual's employment record. Typical falsifications: The individuals don't hold the jobs described; their salaries were not as high as claimed; major difficulties with superiors are completely covered up.'

There is a big difference between falsifying your answers and the tactics outlined in this book. I will summarize them for you.

Remember them and apply them in your interviews. The results will surprise you.

- Never disclose any negative information about yourself voluntarily.
- When asked about your weaknesses, mistakes and other negative information, use the least detrimental case as an example and quickly switch to the corrective action you've taken, improvements and strong points in that area.
- Always listen for clues that will tell what the interviewers want to hear and tell them exactly that. If this calls for 'modifying' the truth, try to look at it from a different perspective. If you haven't actually done something, but know how to do it, transform your theoretical answers into the actual experience. Employers are seldom interested in 'would do' or 'could do' answers. They want details about your specific experience. Don't let them down. If they are happy with your answer, what difference does the fact that you haven't actually done it make? None for them, because you know how to do it and could do it if needed, and big for you, because it can get you the job you want!

# 01

# what are employers looking for?

**In this chapter you will learn:**
- about today's job market
- how to identify the qualities sought by an employer
- how to research a potential employer
- how to prepare a résumé and write an application letter

# When giants learn to dance: the challenging times ahead

The Anglo-Saxon world (the UK, USA, Canada, Australia, New Zealand) has been alternating through states of stagnation and mini-boom, through on-off, semi-permanent recession and patchy recoveries. After the boom decades of the 1960s and 1970s and over-borrowing and overspending trends in the 1980s, the restructuring, downsizing and reengineering 1990s brought a sobering cold shower to many job hunters.

## Employers

Energetic companies these days make it hard to get hired. They deliberately understaff their operations and use the contract work force and part-time employees to cater for peak periods in the business cycle. Recruitment professionals develop detailed selection criteria for each and every position and pay special attention to employing the right people.

The balance of power has shifted completely in favour of the employers. With an average of 40–60 applicants for most professional positions and more than 100 for other jobs, guess who is dictating the terms?

The global lack of vision and strategic planning on the part of the employers is obvious. They take on new people during the upsurges in business, then they put them off again when the business starts to decline. This practice is augmented by the common 'last in, first out' practice, which can leave job seekers with erratic-looking résumés and seriously damage their prospects of gaining employment.

The buyer's market is enabling employers to dictate the terms and freeze (or even reduce) salaries and available benefits. To save money, more and more companies are hiring from the 'bottom of the stack' instead of from the top. By doing that, they are not getting top value for their money: 10% higher salary could mean 100% higher performance.

Robert Townsend says in his best-seller *Up the Organization* (highly recommended):

> *The trouble with personnel experts is that they use gimmicks borrowed from manufacturing: inventories, replacement charts, recruiting, selecting, indoctrinating and training machinery, job rotation, and appraisal*

*programs. And this manufacturing of men is about as effective as Dr. Frankenstein was. As McGregor points out, the sounder approach is agricultural. Provide the climate and proper nourishment and let the people grow themselves. They'll amaze you.*

The current trends among employers are emphasizing more flexible hiring methods, in order to find multi-skilled, adaptable employees who will assume responsibility and accept rapid changes in the work force.

## Employees

High unemployment has an impact on the way employees behave. It creates a timid and compliant work force. They fear their employers and the possibility of losing their jobs. This phenomenon is primarily noticeable in less unionized professions.

To keep our jobs, we have to work harder, longer hours (as much as necessary to effectively accomplish the tasks) and perform virtually any task we were trained for, and all that for the same or less money. So-called 'staff' employees are the hardest hit. In most cases they are not paid for overtime, are not protected by unions, are expected to be loyal to their employer, to put in long hours, keep their heads down and generally be happy just to be employed. So much for fairness and motivation.

The prevailing feeling in today's society is one of disappointment. More and more people are facing the cold reality of unemployment, reduced standard of living and very marginal fulfilment of their dreams. Educational standards are lower and the standard of workmanship and services is slipping. Jobs are scarce and many careers have stalled or have been disrupted by retrenchments, redundancies and lay-offs.

## Restructuring

Restructuring efforts are viewed by employers as the first step towards developing a productive and reliable work force and abandoning restricted work practices and counter-progressive pro-union policies. Such practices and inefficiencies have been eroding economies for decades and significantly contributed to the severity of recession in the early 1990s.

Restructuring of the work force is resulting in much greater emphasis on multi-skilled workers and less on specific credentials and narrowly defined jobs. Transferable skills, such as oral and written communication, interpersonal skills and people-management skills, are gaining importance in the eyes of employers. Because of the difficulty in predicting future trends in the economy and labour market, flexibility and willingness to change are viewed by employers as highly desirable qualities.

Most employers will never employ staff at the levels experienced before the last recession. Some jobs have disappeared, and when the economy picks up, employment will have to be found elsewhere: the old jobs will have changed or won't exist. Voluntary redundancy schemes are gaining popularity among employers who are trying to change the structure of the jobs and decrease the number of employees.

One current trend should be mentioned here. Voluntary or forced redundancy payments are perceived as highly attractive by many employees, who are falling over each other to take the money and hit the road. The number of people wanting to take the packages usually exceeds by far the number of packages available. A possible explanation is that most people believe that it's better to be retrenched now, with a nice payment in their pocket, than to be sacked without any severance pay in a few months' time, when the crisis deepens. I couldn't agree more, but the more important issue here is the *employers'* point of view. Their strategies, policies and philosophies reflect in the hiring process and will directly or indirectly affect you and your future prospects in the job market.

> *Times are tough and will get even tougher. This calls for immediate and drastic action on everybody's part. Employers are getting lean and mean. You'd better follow that path too.*

# Career and job security

In the West, which generally operates according to the principle of supply and demand (either the real one or the artificially created one), the following factors determine how much we get paid:

- The demand for the type of job we do.
- How well we do our jobs.
- How difficult it would be to replace us.

As one of the results of the rapid changes in the way modern companies operated in the harsh economic climate in the late 1980s and early 1990s, long-term employment is rapidly disappearing, leaving those who are unprepared for such a change in total confusion. You simply cannot rely on your employer to take care of you until you retire.

Therefore, the only security you can count on has to come from within yourself. It is based on your knowledge, skills and know-how. To succeed in life you have to take time and make an effort to improve your education and acquire skills that are in demand. In today's business climate one point has to be emphasized:

### *There is no such thing as a secure job!*

Some naive players in the job game think that their jobs are 'for life'. This sense of security comes from the perceived balance of power that existed in the past. They (falsely) presume that:

- Their jobs won't change.
- Their jobs will always exist.
- The employer will feel grateful for their (the employee's) achievements in the past.
- Their employer will take care of their careers, promote them and reward for a job well done.
- If they lose their job, their employer will re-employ them as soon as the hard times are over.

The reality is very different. In today's world the employer is interested only in profits and returns to shareholders and investors. He is too busy to think about you and your family. If things start to go wrong, for whatever reason, in the best case you will be given a few weeks' notice – that is the only loyalty you can expect from your employer.

For us ordinary mortals, the only comforting thing in the whole story is the fact that everybody is in the same boat, from cleaner to CEO. Whole lines of management are disappearing; professionals (engineers, lawyers, accountants) are being retrenched; the axe falls on all layers of the corporate structure.

So, you had better start to like living dangerously. If you don't already enjoy it, force yourself to accept challenge and uncertainty. Try to conquer the symptoms of an 'ostrich syndrome'. Don't bury your head in the sand! You can use it for better purposes – to observe the job market, note trends, make conclusions and plan your actions.

## Testing the job-market

Instead of spending hours on Saturdays and Sundays reading the sport pages of your daily newspaper, devote an hour or two to scanning employment advertisements, even if you are employed. That could give you the right perspective. At least it could give you an idea about what's happening in the job market. You might be pleasantly surprised if you discover that there is a healthy demand for people with qualifications and experience similar to yours.

You could even go a step further. If you are not sure about your value or your career prospects, apply for a few jobs just to 'probe' the market.

Some less reputable employers do this too. Although they are not allowed (by law) to use this method of 'market research', employers sometimes advertise for non-existent positions to get a better idea about the market for certain groups of employees. That helps them in salary reviews, in dealings with unions and in other strategies used to keep the balance of power in their favour.

You have an advantage over your employer in this area, because it is perfectly legal to apply for a job without any intention of accepting the offer. Even if you are not thinking about changing jobs, this exercise can give you a sense of reality and assist you in putting a price-tag on yourself. You could be worth more than you think!

## Managing your career

*Fortune* magazine columnist Walter Kiechel advises job hunters to jump at jobs at other companies whenever the opportunity arises, because when they are forced to leave their present employers those jobs might not be there. For him, the 'New Employment Contract' holds that:

> *Hereinafter, the employee will assume full responsibility for his own career – for keeping his qualifications up to date, for getting himself moved to the next position at the right time, for salting away funds for retirement, and, most daunting of all, for achieving job satisfaction. The company, while making no promises, will endeavour to provide a conducive environment, economic exigencies permitting.*

So, if security no longer comes from being employed, where does it come from? From being *employable*! Employability security is the new term that is becoming increasingly popular in a post-entrepreneurial world. It means that you should:

- Accumulate knowledge, skills and a reputation that can easily be transferred to other companies and invested in new opportunities.
- Try to master 'portable skills', ones that will be in demand because they could easily be applied in various corporate environments.
- Base your career management on your résumé. Ask yourself about every assignment, every project – 'How will this experience benefit my career prospects?' and 'How is it going to look on my résumé?'
- Stay in touch with influential people outside your present employer, people who can help you in finding a job should the need arise. Cultivate your relationships with recruiters and employment agents. You'll need them to help you in your job-hunting efforts.
- Remain visible, mobile and credible. Do not overspecialize. Keep all your options open.

# The ideal employee: dream of a genetic engineer

*As a personnel management trainee, I was told the perfect advertisement was the one which drew one reply and that was from the ideal candidate.*

Len Peach, *The Times*, 29 August 1985

## Skills in demand

If you ask ten employers to define an ideal employee, it is very likely that you will get ten different answers. Each interviewer has his or her own ideas about the person they would like to employ. The traits that are extremely important in some positions might not be relevant for other jobs. To illustrate these differences we'll use a computer programmer, secretary and design engineer for examples. For each of these positions the critical success factors differ.

## Computer programmer

- Knowledge of the particular computing environment (OS/2, DOS, UNIX, CPM, Windows ...).
- A working knowledge of operating systems, programming languages and software packages.
- Attention to detail.
- Mathematical/analytical skills.
- Appropriate work standards.
- Good communication skills (especially written).
- Appropriate typing skills.

## Secretary

- Good typing speed (words per minute).
- Shorthand skills.
- Ability to use word-processing packages and personal computers.
- Interpersonal and communication skills.
- Good grammar, editing and proofreading skills.
- Sensitivity.
- Initiative, ability to learn.
- Co-operation and team-work.

## Design engineer

- Knowledge of relevant standards, regulations and work practices.
- Ability to work alone and in a team environment.
- Good technical knowledge of the required discipline.
- Drafting skills.
- Estimating and budgeting skills.
- Attention to detail.
- High work standards.
- Effective oral and written communication skills.

Despite the differences, there are some qualities that are highly regarded by employers and therefore sought after. With those qualities in mind, the ideal employee should be:

- Mature and responsible.
- Competent.
- Trained and experienced.
- A good communicator.
- A good motivator.

- A self-starter.
- Able to work alone and in a team.
- Loyal.
- Mentally and physically healthy.
- Easy to work with.
- Highly ethical and of high integrity.
- Self-motivated.

## Interviewers' fears

To be successful in the interview, you have to realize that interviewers are almost as nervous, anxious and confused as the applicants themselves. By asking each question, they try to find an answer to one of their fears and concerns. You, the candidate, have to frame your answers accordingly, address those aspects and convince employers that their fears are without foundation – in other words, that you are a good investment of their time and money.

What are the major employers' fears?

1 Employee won't be able to do the job, due to lack of necessary skills or experience.
2 Employee won't be self-motivated.
3 Employee will frequently be on sick leave.
4 Employee will stay around for only a short time and resign as soon as a better opportunity comes up.
5 Employee will take too long to learn the job and to become a profitable investment.
6 Employee won't get along well with co-workers and the management.
7 Employee will do only the absolute minimum he or she can get away with, rather than maximum he or she is capable of.
8 Employee will bring discredit upon the boss – and the whole department.

There are three basic groups of people: some people make things happen, some watch things happen and some wonder what happened. Employers want to employ people who make things happen, not passive bystanders.

*In your answers, project the 'I'm a person of action' attitude.*

## What do employers expect from you?

To be able to present yourself in the best light and to maximize your chances of getting a job or a promotion, you have to understand what your prospective employers expect from you. The examples I will give are generic and broad but all other, more specific, expectations will be based on these major themes. Once you know what the major theme of the play is, as any good actor, you should be able to improvise your answers!

- Solve my problems. Make my life easier and make me look good in the eyes of others.
- Speak my language. Level with me and become a part of my team.
- Avoid surprises. Be predictable and trustworthy, make me feel comfortable.
- Don't tell me what I cannot do. Tell me how to do what I want to do.
- Take the initiative. Display leadership and take action.
- Innovate. Offer new and better ways of doing things.
- Be honest and sincere. Keep confidential issues confidential. Establish trust.
- Give it your best shot. Deliver what you promised you would. Close that credibility gap.
- Show sincere interest in my problems. Be seen, talk to people, ask questions, give them answers.

## Job descriptions and selection criteria

When preparing for a job interview, the first prerequisite is to identify the qualities most sought after by that particular employer. You should base your performance on these factors in order to impress the head hunters.

Very useful tools for doing this are job descriptions and selection criteria. Some big companies use them, but public companies and government departments are particularly inclined towards them. Most applicants have to address the selection criteria in their applications. The same applies for the interview.

By making selection criteria available to applicants, employers try to scare off the less qualified or less experienced candidates. Accidentally, while succeeding at that most of the time, they also help some shrewd professional interviewees to frame their interview presentations accordingly.

# Doing your homework on employers: knowing me, knowing you

*The two most important things in any business do not appear on its balance sheet – they are its People and its Reputation.*

Henry Ford

Ideally, you should start doing your research on a potential employer even before you send your résumé to them. That way you can frame your application to suit each employer's circumstances, their way of thinking and operating and, most importantly, their selection criteria. If you get invited for an interview, the importance of getting to know the employer skyrockets.

*As you expand your knowledge of the employer, the balance of power shifts in your favour.*

If you are able to show the interviewer that you have done some research on their company and that you know a lot about their operations, they are likely to think: 'If he went to all that trouble to find out details about us before the interview, can you imagine what he could do for us if we employ him? This is the person we want on our team!'

You can show your knowledge through pertinent, implicit statements, smart and appropriate questions and properly framed answers to questions. Don't try to 'look smart' or convince the interviewers that you have done research on their companies. Let them realize that themselves.

The question in front of us now is 'how to approach the whole investigation process?' By following the basic steps outlined below.

1 Information gathering. This is the most tedious and time-consuming task, but it pays high interest!
2 Screening the facts and selecting the relevant information. Easier than the previous task and much more interesting.
3 Using the relevant facts in framing your answers. The best answers (given in Chapter 6) should be expanded and modified to suit your particular case and each employer. Always keep in mind one rule: *tell them what they want to hear.*

There are various methods and tactics that could help you in doing your homework on potential employers. Some will prove invaluable, for the information you gather may make a difference between success and failure at the interview. Let's take a quick look at the sources of information and methods of using it.

## Scanning the available literature

The time spent in a library could prove your best investment in your employment search. Trade and financial magazines and publications are excellent sources of information. Annual reports, brochures, pamphlets and newsletters published by the company could be even more valuable.

As a general suggestion, I would advise you to establish your own databank on major employers in your field. Collect all articles from newspapers and magazines and other printed materials, job advertisements, etc. Establish a filing system for easy reference and updating.

## Using your friends and acquaintances as sources of information

Friends and relatives can provide you with specific 'inside' information about the companies they work for, or through them you can meet people that work for the companies you are interviewing with. Inside information is most valuable and would certainly give you an edge over other candidates.

However, at the interview, do not mention friends or acquaintances who work for that company. You don't how know good (or bad) the personal relationship between the interviewer and your friend is, so you could do your prospects serious damage.

## Using business contacts

If you plan to stay within the industry you are already in, business contacts could provide you with the same, or even more detailed, inside information. They will know most corporate games, plans and developments, so if you have a good relationship with them, they might dispense information to you. Always foster good relationships with your former employers, customers, suppliers, etc. You never know when you are going to need them.

# Contact the prospective employer

Before your interview, contact the receptionist or the interviewer's secretary by phone – or go and see them personally. The best time for this is when arranging the interview. Use the opportunity to find out about the interviewer(s) – name, title, position, background, etc. Formulate your questions carefully, so you don't sound too pushy or nosy.

Try to establish friendly contact with secretaries and receptionists. Quite often interviewers ask them for an opinion on the candidates or about their impression of applicants when they approach the desk.

The people you talk to on the phone are often not the ones who will interview you. If they ask why you want to know those details, you can say that you don't want to appear unprepared at the interview and that you don't want to waste anybody's time if you're not qualified. Of course, you don't want to waste *your* precious time if you're over-qualified, either.

The best tactic would be to go to see the receptionist or secretary in person. They usually appreciate a little chat if you show genuine interest in them and their company. It is very easy to dismiss a faceless voice over the phone: in a face-to-face meeting, they are more likely to help you.

The worst possible feeling at the interview is not knowing who your interviewers are, the roles they play in the company or what they expect from the candidates. In most cases the first and last time most job applicants hear their names and titles is at the beginning of the interview, when they introduce themselves. Most candidates are either very nervous at that stage or try to make a good impression on the interviewers, so they concentrate on how to introduce themselves and don't get the names right. *Never* start an interview without knowing who your interviewers are and where they fit in the company's structure.

# Classifying information

The information you obtain from the sources listed above will cover the whole range of areas and aspects of the prospective employer. Your next task will be to put the available data into categories, which will enable you to systematize your knowledge of the employer and use the facts you collected to your advantage. So what areas should you be looking at? What questions do you have to find answers for? Here are some of the most important ones.

## Services and products produced by the company

- Does the company provide services, products or both?
- What type of products or services?
- How many different products or services are produced?
- Which products or services are the most profitable or have the greatest potential?
- How are the products produced or services provided? What manufacturing methods are used?
- What quality-control techniques are used?

## The company's customers and markets

- Who are the company's main customers?
- How good is the relationship between the company and its customers?
- What is the history of that relationship? What are the present and future trends?
- What are the firm's plans in the areas of marketing, new markets or expanding the existing ones?

## Organizational aspects of the company

- How is the company organized? What is the function of each department?
- How many layers of management does the company have? What are they?
- What are the main areas of responsibility for each level?
- Which departments generate profit? Which ones are not so successful?
- What are the opportunities for advancement through the ranks?

## Details about the position you have applied for

- Who does the position report to?
- How long has the position been open?
- Who were the previous employees in the position?
- Is it a new position? If it is, why was it created?
- What are the opportunities for promotion?
- What happened to previous incumbents? Were they retrenched, promoted or have they resigned?

### The company's history and future plans
- When was the company established?
- Does the company show steady growth over the years?
- Is the company expanding its business or stagnating?
- Who are the major shareholders (if the company is listed on the stock market)?

# Résumés and application letters

Once you've finished your research on the employer you are interested in, you can start writing your résumé. If you have already compiled it, all you have to do is to tailor it to suit the employer and the position you are going to apply for. Job seekers usually don't perceive modifying their résumé as a crucial step in getting an invitation to a job interview but nothing could be further from the truth.

How do you arouse interest in a person who has never seen you or spoken to you? How do you relate the most important facts of your life in a matter of minutes? How do you present your achievements and outline your strengths on a couple of pages?

By compiling an effective and attractive résumé. Your résumé is everything: your school record, diplomas, certificates, degrees, experience, employment history, knowledge, strengths, interests, goals and much more, all condensed into an explosive compound whose only purpose is to knock recruiters off their feet and make them want you badly.

You have probably read some of the great old masterpieces from the past, when the only way to win a woman's heart was through romantic letters, poetry and an occasional red rose. This is exactly how you can win an employer's heart. Not by sending them red roses, but through potent and powerful words in your résumé and application letter.

Your résumé is the most powerful selling tool at your disposal. Invest time and money in its preparation and keep it updated. Its only purpose is to secure a job interview.

When applying for a job, always make that extra effort and find out the name of the person to whom you are sending your résumé and application letter. A title is not enough. By

addressing a person by their name you break the inti[m]
barrier. A person's name is the most important word i[n]
everybody's vocabulary. Everybody wants to see their name
written and referred to: it makes them feel valued.

Using names is not enough, however. Use simple and effective
language, without clichés, stock phrases and formalities. Write
the same way you would talk to that person if he was standing
before you. Don't try to impress too much. Be brief. Avoid going
into too many details and don't boost your achievements. You
do that at the interview.

## How to prepare your résumé – the rules of the game

1 Prepare it yourself. Don't use agencies. Do, however, use word-processing software and a laser printer if you have access to them. To the average employer, presentation is often more important than substance. Sad, but true.

2 Get somebody else with a good knowledge of English grammar and style to proofread it. The more times, the better.

3 Ask as many relevant people as possible to give you their opinion on the content, quality and style of your résumé.

4 Use high-quality stationery, preferably creamy or light blue in colour. Although white is the norm, you want your résumé to stand out. Avoid screaming colours. Subtle pastels or sky-blue high-quality bond stands out just enough to be noticed and remembered.

5 Don't lie or exaggerate your accomplishments. Honesty is the best policy as far as résumés are concerned (interviews are slightly different, as we are going to see later).

6 Use words that project an image of a person who takes action, assumes responsibility and achieves results: designed, calculated, established, started, initiated, introduced, managed, supervised, monitored, investigated, trained, achieved, increased, saved …

7 The following facts *don't* have a place on your résumé (so make sure you leave them out): your present or past salaries, expected salary, the names of your references, a photograph of yourself, your nationality, height, weight, eye colour, names of your spouse and children.

information that you may or may not include is
, your marital status, hobbies and outside interests. I
ecommend you leave all of them out. These facts have
g to do with your ability to do a job; they are totally
ant and may serve as an 'invitation' to some sort of
nination by employers.

objective is another sticky point. Many job hunting
books say it's a 'must'. I wouldn't recommend it. Should you
decide to include it, make sure it is brief, concise and placed
at the very beginning of the résumé.

## Action words

The words you use in your résumé should be relatively short,
action oriented, concise and unambiguous. They will help you
project an image of a results-driven doer, action-oriented
achiever. Every word of action will say what you've done in the
past and translate into what you could do, if hired. These are
some examples:

---

generated directed scheduled monitored maximized
co-ordinated optimized instructed taught
demonstrated established guided introduced
eliminated reduced completed controlled
implemented conducted accomplished revised
modified managed supervised administered
designed built provided researched analysed
evaluated performed motivated delivered trained
expedited created invented composed developed
founded solved proved negotiated planned
launched organized structured increased
expanded saved streamlined improved sold
maintained

# The right and wrong ways to do it

## The worst résumé writers' mistakes

### Too long

The information provided is not concise, relevant or captivating. It resembles a fairy tale rather than a direct, straight-to-the-point communication medium. There are many redundant words and information is often repeated.

### Too short

There isn't enough information to enable the employer to properly evaluate the candidate. In some cases, long employment records cannot possibly be condensed down to one or two pages, which is the norm for résumés. It is perfectly acceptable to produce a longer résumé if the circumstances require such an approach.

### Poor presentation

The résumé is sloppy, untidy, poorly designed graphically or poorly reproduced (photocopied). The paper is folded too many times and resembles a bus ticket, not a professional presentation.

### Spelling and grammar errors

The first impression spelling and grammar errors create is lack of attention to detail and lack of concentrated effort, both of which are serious flaws in any occupation. The recruiter gets the feeling that a candidate isn't very keen to create a good impression and get the job.

### Too slick

It is obvious that the résumé has been prepared by a professional. It may also be boastful and some exaggeration is suspected, seriously undermining the candidate's credibility.

# The right way

Stephanie Haber
5 Great James Street
London, WC1N 3DA
020 7938 1055 (Home) 020 7975 3364 (W/H)

| | |
|---|---|
| **Personal:** | Born 24 September 1974 |
| **Education:** | BSc in accounting, University of London, 1996, MBA in Technology Management, University of London, 1999 |

**Experience:**

Jan 1998–present
: Logitech Consulting Company
*Contracts Officer*
In charge of the Contracts Department. Responsible for the negotiation and administration of contracts, liaison with clients, tender preparation and approval. Developed a project status reporting system using networked Macintosh computers. Attended courses in Quality Control and became proficient in the ISO 9000 series of quality standards.
Proficient in the use of word processing, spreadsheet, data base and other PC-based software packages.

Dec 1996–Jan 1998
: Specialized Engineering Co.
*Project Controller*
Responsible for the administration of projects and contracts for a toolmaking engineering company. Established internal quality control procedures for contract administration tasks. Achieved cost savings in the order of £300,000 per year. Developed and successfully implemented a new computerized system for cost monitoring and control.

May 1996–Dec 1996
: Smith and Partners – Public Accountants
*Graduate Trainee*
Responsibilities included general accounting work, preparation of tax returns, auditing of clients' accounts and internal procedures, budget and cash flow preparations. After the initial training, appointed account supervisor for two major clients in the engineering sector.

| | |
|---|---|
| **Membership of professional bodies:** | British Institute of Certified Accountants |
| **Other interests:** | Computers, netball, winter sports |
| **References:** | Available on request after the interview |

# The wrong way

Stephanie Haber
5 Great James Street
London, WC1N 3DA
020 7938 1055 (Home) 020 7975 3364 (W/H)

**Objective:** A well-paid administrative position with an engineering or construction company in the inner London area. Will consider short assignments outside London, but only if the salary offered is at least 20% above my present remuneration.

**Personal:**Born 24 September 1974, Height: 169 cm, Weight: 56 kg, Eyes: blue, Hair: brown. Happily married to John, no children. Health: excellent (except an occasional migraine and allergies)

**Hobbies and interests:** Computers, netball, winter sports

| **Education:** | 1992–1996 | BSc in accounting, University of London |
| | 1996–1999 | MBA in Technology Management, University of London |

## Employment history:

1996–1996 Smith and Partners – Public Accountants
*Graduate Trainee*
Performed general accounting work, preparation of tax returns, and checking of clients' accounts. Also performed budget and cash flow preparations under close supervision. After the initial training, resigned and joined Specialized Engineering Company which offered higher salary and better conditions.

1996–1998 Specialized Engineering Co.
*Project controller*
Performed the administration of projects and contracts for a small toolmaking engineering company. Established basic internal quality control procedures for contract administration tasks. Participated in the development and implementation of a new computerized system for cost monitoring and control. Left because of personal differences with the Project Supervisor.

1998 until now Logitech Consulting Company
*Contracts officer*
Hired to oversee the operation of the Contracts Department, which included negotiation and administration of contracts, liaison with clients, tender preparation and approval. Developed a project status reporting system using networked Macintosh computers. Attended courses in Quality Control. Due to company's downsizing efforts, became redundant in January 1994.

**References:**
Peter Seymour, Senior Partner, Smith and Partners
Alison Jones, Project Supervisor, Specialized Engineering Co.
Michael Taylor, Engineering Administration Manager, Logitech Consulting Company

### Analysing the mistakes

1 The objective is demanding and shows bad taste. It lacks modesty and moderation. It creates a very bad first impression.

2 There are too many personal details. Height, weight, the colour of candidate's eyes and hair, husband's name, health details are all no-nos. Even marital status could be omitted.

3 There is no need to specify the exact periods of study. Graduating year usually suffices.

4 On the other hand, employment experience requires months to be specified, not just years of employment. 1996–1998 could mean January 1996 until December 1999, which is almost four years, or it may mean December 1996 until January 1999, which is just over two years! This is a very common trick used by job hoppers and despised by employers.

5 Employment history doesn't sound very nice: it refers to the past tense. 'Employment achievements' or simply 'employment' is much better.

6 Employment details are always listed in reverse, chronological order, starting with the most current position held and ending with the first job you had.

7 It isn't necessary to list references on your résumé. It takes valuable space that could be better used for other purposes, such as listing your achievements and accomplishments.

8 The reasons for leaving should *not* be put on a résumé. It is much wiser to discuss them at a job interview (but only if asked by the interviewer). That way you can explain exactly what happened, how and why. If simply stated on a résumé, certain facts (personal differences, retrenchments, etc.) will certainly create negative impressions.

## Writing application letters

There are some general rules you should follow when applying for a job and writing application letters. If you follow them, you may find yourself in a new job sooner than you think. This doesn't mean that you have to follow the rules blindly to get a job. It only means that if you do get a job without doing your homework properly you got it not because of your efforts, but despite them.

## Rule 1: research and investigation

When applying for a job that was advertised in the press, before writing your application letter study the job advertisement in depth. Analyse the words, the order of sentences, the syntax. Try to read between the lines and get a feeling about the person who wrote the ad and the company's way of thinking. What personal and professional characteristics are important to the employer? What type of person are they looking for? What are the minimum requirements (*absolute musts*) when qualifications and experience are concerned? What are the 'nice to have' attributes? Where do you fit in that description? Which ones of your strong points could you emphasize in your application?

Only once you've answered all these questions can you say 'I've done my homework properly, let's write the application that's going to win me a job interview.' Notice the word 'win'. Your application has to be a *winning* application, your résumé a *winning* résumé. Writing application letters is like painting: the longest, most tedious and monotonous tasks are information gathering and research. They can be likened to surface preparation: cleaning, sanding, filling, sanding, cleaning, priming. Then comes the painting, the brush strokes. The compilation of your résumé and application letter are possibly the easiest and quickest tasks of all.

## Rule 2: language and style

Your application letter and résumé serve only one purpose: to get you invited for a job interview. They are the only presentation tools you have before the job interview, so make sure you use them properly. Avoid hackneyed phrases and clichés in your application letter. Your language should be alive and vivid and should attract the reader's attention. Spelling mistakes and grammatical or syntax errors are cardinal sins and will almost certainly cause your application to end up in the waste basket.

It helps to have somebody to proofread your application documents and give you honest and unbiased feedback on the quality, clarity and style of your writing. Two pairs of eyes see more than one, so don't hesitate to show your draft letters to people who are willing to help.

## Rule 3: presentation

Give your application letter and résumé a nice look. Use only top-quality paper. Print it out on a laser printer or a good-quality inkjet. Be conservative with colours. Black or dark blue for text and white or light pastel colours for paper are the best. Use fonts that are easy to read. Avoid fancy styles and try not to use more than two styles: one for headings, one for paragraphs. Do, however, use italics and bold for the facts and achievements that need emphasizing.

When you mail your résumé, don't fold it or staple the pages together. Send it with your application letter in an A4-sized envelope. This projects a truly professional image. An application folded two or three times looks just like a piece of junk mail and usually ends up in the same place: the waste basket.

*Three things are of paramount importance for creating a great résumé: presentation, presentation and presentation.*

Before you seal the envelope, make sure two things are not missing: your signature and a copy of your résumé. You would be surprised how many times applicants forget to sign the letter of application. Some even forget to enclose their résumé.

## Rule 4: follow up

When you send your job application to a prospective employer, make a note in your diary and keep photocopies of all correspondence. This is especially important if you have a couple of different versions of your résumé, tailored to suit each particular application. That way you won't be caught unprepared at the interview should the interviewer, based on the information supplied on your résumé, ask you some specific question or need clarification.

After a week or so, telephone the employer just to confirm that they have received your application. Don't leave anything to chance. Display initiative. Find out how long the short-listing of applicants is going to take, so you can prepare yourself for an interview, should you be on the short-list. Make a plan for your interview preparations and stick to it.

The biggest mistake you can make in job hunting is not to follow up your application. Always remind employers of your candidacy and project keen interest in the progress of your application. Most employers will appreciate your resourcefulness and systematic, organized approach to career issues.

## Rule 5: the method

There are a few basic methods you can use to get your application and your résumé into the hands of a prospective employer. Let's start with the latest.

### E-mail:

E-mail is becoming a preferred method of communication, not just among computer buffs. It has found its place among professionals, students and other groups and sectors of the community.

Communication by e-mail is quick, personal and, above all, confidential. No uninvited prying eyes here: your application is opened by the person it is addressed to. However, there are pitfalls.

1 Personnel departments and managers in user departments are likely to get dozens, sometimes hundreds of e-mail applications. Everybody is doing it. Your application *has to stand out* in any (positive) way you can make it stand out; this way it won't!

2 Sooner or later, the receiving employer will print out your résumé and your application. They will not put much effort into formatting it and the printed version may look cluttered, confusing, unprofessional. Why jeopardize your chances? Print it out yourself (in colour, if possible – good colour ink-jet printers can be bought for less than £200) and forget e-mail.

3 It is somehow much more difficult to spot errors on a computer screen. How many times were you satisfied with your résumé or application letter, then, after printing it out, just before enclosing it in an envelope, discovered a major blunder, omission or spelling mistake? Once you press the send button on your e-mail package, your only chance of avoiding mistakes is gone.

4 Many employers perceive that written, printed applications require more effort and skill than e-mail equivalents. You want to be perceived as industrious and hard working, don't you?

If you cannot live without sending e-mail applications, there is an alternative. Use a word processor to prepare your résumé and application letter then attach them to the main e-mail. At least the formatting problems will be resolved, but then there is the issue of incompatibility between your word-processing software and the recipient's. If you thought personnel departments work in mysterious ways, what would you say about their software?

If I were you, I would forget e-mail as a method of sending your applications in!

**Fax:**

Faxing is another option. The main drawback again is presentation. Most corporations still use old thermal technology and flimsy, light-sensitive paper. Not even Claudia Schiffer's face would look good on that. The paper curls, the pages get mixed up with other faxes (or lost altogether), the resolution is poor, so your letters are jagged and your paragraphs are crooked. Again, in my opinion, a major no-no.

Remember, applying for a job is like a seduction. Would you fax a love poem to your sweetheart, or would you present it in person on a nice, creamy parchment paper, wrapped with love? Employers are human, therefore they can be impressed in the same way!

If delivering your application in person is not practical or would be too expensive, consider using a courier service. Think like a guerrilla fighter. Instead of paying, say, £1 in postage for a normal A4 envelope, pay £5 for a hand-delivered, signature-required courier service. If they have to sign for it, and a delivery person is delivering just one letter – yours – then it must be something important. And you bet it is – for you.

# Good and bad application letters

## *This* is how to do it

Stephanie Haber
5 Great James Street
London, WC1N 3DA
020 7938 1055 (Home)       020 7975 3364 (W/H)

2 February 2000

Mr Nigel Pettigrove
Personnel Manager
Booth, Smith and Partners
29 Abingdon Road
London W8 6AL

Dear Mr Pettigrove

With reference to your advertisement in The Times on 28
January 2000, I would like to express my strong interest in
the position of Senior Contract Administrator.

After seven years in various administrative positions in the
consulting sector, I am ready for new challenges. I am sure my
education, theoretical and practical knowledge and experience
in project management, negotiation and administration of
contracts will benefit your engineering consultancy.

My strong analytical and technical skills, and my ability to
work with people and on urgent and demanding tasks should
enable me to start achieving results in the shortest possible
time. I have had experience in liaison with clients, vendors
and Government and statutory bodies, in budget preparations,
cost control, supervision of office personnel, coordinating,
planning and report writing and presentation.

The current economic climate requires an innovative and
rational approach to project management and engineering in
general. I understand all aspects of client service,
reliability and safety aspects of engineering, as well as the
implementation of Total Quality Control methods. Most of all,
I understand people, how to work with them in a result-
orientated team environment.

A copy of my résumé and qualifications is enclosed for your
reference. Should you require further information do not
hesitate to contact me at any time. I would welcome the
opportunity to meet with you to discuss this position and my
background in more detail, and to explore the ways I could
contribute to the ongoing success of your firm.

I appreciate your consideration and look forward to hearing
from you.

Yours sincerely,
Stephanie Haber
Encl.

# This is how *not* to do it

Stephanie Haber
5 Great James Street
London, WC1N 3DA
020 7938 1055 (Home)      020 7975 3364 (W/H)

2 February 2000

Personnel Manager
Booth, Smith and Partners
29 Abingdon Road
London W8 6AL

Dear Sir

I am reading with great interest your advertisement in 'The
Times'. I would like to apply for the job of Senior Contract
Administrator. I have been working on similar jobs for more
than seven years now, so joining a prosperous company such as
yours would be a nice change.

Although my background is not in engineering, I am sure I
could handle the task outlined in your advertisement without
major hassles. Being a Libra, my pleasant personality and
popularity in the office would more than compensate for my
lack of engineering qualifications.

I am looking for a challenging position with a major
consulting firm in the engineering or construction sector,
which doesn't involve travel and regular overtime work. I just
got married and am planning to have my first child soon. I
would consider relocating, should an attractive package be
offered, especially the health insurance coverage.

Currently I am unemployed and have been using this time to
learn French and improve my career prospects.

I have enclosed a copy of my résumé and qualifications. If you
require further information do not hesitate to contact me at
any time. If you think my qualifications and experience would
be suitable for this opening, I would be glad to attend an
interview.

Thank you for your time.

Yours sincerely,

Stephanie Haber

Encl.

## Analysing the mistakes

1 The second letter is addressed to the Personnel Manager. It is much better to address it to the actual person and to avoid 'Dear Sir' or 'Dear Sirs' salutations. It's much easier to create a friendly and intimate feeling when addressing a person by name.

2 Almost every sentence begins with 'I'. Avoid this as much as you can. An application letter should tell the employer what you could do for them, not what you want for yourself! Statements such as 'I am reading with great interest' or 'I would like' put people off and should not be used.

3 The fact that you are currently unemployed should be omitted and the reason should be explained at the interview (but only if you are asked to do so).

4 The second paragraph emphasizes the lack of engineering qualifications and tries to compensate for that by mentioning applicant's star sign and personality traits. It would be funny if it wasn't tragic.

5 The third paragraph projects a picture of someone who cares only about her spare time, her family life and the employment benefits. If I were the personnel manager reading this letter, I wouldn't go past this point. The lights would go off, the curtain would come down. This is a typical 'waste basket' case.

6 The ending paragraph is doubtful. The applicant herself isn't sure if her qualifications and experience are adequate for the job. She leaves it to the personnel manager to decide if that is the case, instead of charging ahead with self-confidence and proclaiming 'I would welcome the opportunity to explore the ways I could help your firm in its ongoing success'. It makes a world of difference!

# 02

## what can you offer?

**In this chapter you will learn:**
- how to evaluate yourself
- how to eliminate your weaknesses and neutralize obstacles
- how to improve your interviewing skills and performance

# Personal audit (your +/– sheet)

*To know where you are going and how to get there, you must first know yourself.*

> Vincent Clement Stone, *The Success System*
> *That Never Fails*

People have a surprising tendency towards self-deception. They usually overestimate their strengths and underestimate their weaknesses. They concentrate on successful dealings with others, but forget how to deal properly with themselves. Being smart and astute when dealing with others does not necessarily mean that you are not fooling yourself.

On the other hand, underestimating your strengths and/or overestimating your weaknesses is even worse: that sort of attitude certainly won't help you in job hunting. As always in life, balance should be reached.

*Self-knowledge is the key: whether you design skyscrapers or run the lunch counter, you cannot use your talents to their fullest unless you also know your weaknesses.*

> Mark H. McCormack, *The 110% Solution*

## Job hunters' personalities

Professional psychologists like to group people into 'types' – or should I say 'stereotypes'? Classifying characters into 'bins' helps them make general assumptions about our habits, personalities, attitudes and behaviour.

For illustrative purposes I'll do something similar here. We'll take a look at some typical personalities and their approaches to job hunting and interviewing. You might recognize some of your attributes here. That is the main aim of this exercise – to start you thinking about your own personality, your own good and bad points.

### Straight shooters

Owing to their inherent honesty and high integrity, they always tell the truth and nothing but the truth to interviewers. They don't know how to emphasize their good points and minimize their weaknesses. More often than not, losers in the job game.

### Professionals

They do everything right, from preparation for the interview to the 'Thank you' note afterwards. They know what employers want to hear. The winners in the job game. After reading this book and some practice, you can become a professional, too.

### Con artists

They possess hardly any relevant qualifications or skills for the jobs they apply for but, being masters of interviewing and manipulating people, they land jobs easier than others. Usually, they learn from some less reputable politicians and crook business 'tycoons' but they end up in the same place – the waste basket.

### Epicureans

Epicureans enjoy life to the fullest. They 'work to live' and don't care for overtime or commitment to the company they work for. Not particularly ambitious.

### Workaholics

Opposite to the epicureans. All work and no play make them dull. They sacrifice everything for their work. Of course, employers love them. This breed is on the brink of extinction.

### Machiavellians

Their credo is: 'The end justifies the means.' They could be either professionals or con artists: other types seldom use this sort of philosophy. Machiavellians are high achievers and, while they strive to win, sometimes use and abuse everything and everybody that can help them to get there.

Your task at an interview is to convince the potential employer that you are somewhere between a straight shooter and a workaholic. However, the purpose of this book is to help you become a professional interviewee, no matter which group you belong to or what your philosophy in life is.

## Self-evaluation sheets and how to use them

On the following pages you can find examples of basic self-assessment sheets. Copy them, then write a short evaluation of each particular strength or weakness, as it applies to you. You can use short statements like *OK*, if you are satisfied with a particular skill, *to improve* if you feel the need and room for

improvement in that area, or *very strong* if you hav
outstanding skill. For example:

**Willing to learn**   through courses, on the job – *OK*
**Management skills**   supervisory experience, plan for a management course
**Experience**   two years in accounting, good start
**Able to work under pressure**   yes, on urgent tasks – *OK*
**Takes initiative**   occasionally, not too often – *to improve*
or
**English**   good language skills – *very strong*
**Self-esteem**   generally good, sometimes low – *to improve*
**No work experience**   limited experience, two years
**Low grades in school/university**   good grades – *OK*
**Bad references**   nothing detrimental – *OK*

You can create your own sheets if you find the enclosed ones not suitable, or add your own strengths and weaknesses at the bottom of the sheets. Whatever you do, *be honest with yourself*. Nobody else will see your self-assessment. Keep your sheets in your personal folder in a safe place. As you make progress and improve your skills or eliminate your weaknesses you can change them or fill in new ones.

After the self-evaluation sheets, you'll find an example of a work experience analysis sheet. To prepare yourself for an interview, use the copies of the sheet to analyse your past performance. Use a separate sheet for each major task or project or for a group of smaller interrelated jobs. By doing this evaluation properly, you will make it much easier for yourself later when you prepare your own answers to typical interview questions in Chapter 6.

Again, you can customize the sheet to suit your preferences, or create your own. In this case form is not important, the essence is.

Before your start analysing your past experience and filling your sheets in, read Chapter 6 to get a basic idea about:

- The areas interviewers are interested in.
- Typical interview questions.
- The reasons interviewers ask those questions.
- Model answers, which should be a starting point for your own customized answers.

offer?

02

and 'classifying' your past tasks, experiences ...nts, try to group and evaluate them on the basis ...ctors such as initiative, integrity, ability to learn, ..., planning and control, attention to detail, work ..., etc. The questions in Chapter 6 are based on these ...ions. Your self-analysis should help you come up with ...ples that illustrate each dimension. For example, some of ...more important cases would be:

- When you achieved more than you expected.
- When you failed despite giving your best.
- When you succeeded because you persisted for a period of time.
- When you successfully implemented someone else's idea.
- When you successfully implemented your own idea.
- When you made a difficult decision.
- When you did more than was required.
- When you failed/succeeded because of poor/proper planning.
- When you felt you could have done a better job.
- When you had to go against the rules or policies in order to get a job done or achieve the planned target.

When you finish your objective analysis (be honest with yourself), identify your mistakes and areas for improvement. The last step would be to find a way of emphasizing the things you have done right, covering up the things that went wrong and lessening the impact your mistakes may have on the interviewers.

*Even if it's true, never confess that you did something selfish, silly, foolish, unlawful, unsafe, or that you acted irresponsibly, impulsively, or against the rules. Absolute honesty and frankness are precious commodities, except in a job interview.*

## SELF-EVALUATION SHEET 1
### My strengths and assets:

Independent or team player

Self-starter

Good communication skills

Willing to learn

Management skills

Experienced

Able to work under pressure

Takes initiative

Reliable and responsible

Flexible

Co-operative/easy to work with

Persistent

Decisive

Able to delegate

Thorough (attention to details)

Innovative

Loyal

## SELF-EVALUATION SHEET 2
## My weaknesses and handicaps:

Poor English

Low self-esteem

No work experience

Low grades in school/at University

Bad references from previous employers

Immigrant or minority

Physical or mental handicap

Not enough education

Poor communication skills

Poor interviewing skills

Unsystematic and inefficient

Too specialized

Too much of a generalist

Tendency to procrastinate

Lack of drive/ambitions

Lack of planning

Lack of self-discipline

Poor health

## WORK EXPERIENCE ANALYSIS SHEET

Employer:

Date:

Case:

Situation:

My task:

The outcome (results):

Accomplishments:

Mistakes made:

The cause of those mistakes:

Lessons learned:

# Eliminating your weaknesses and neutralizing obstacles

*I believe the only way to reform people is to kill them.*

Carl Panzram, US mass murderer,
hanged at Fort Leavenworth, 1930

At a job interview, the employer will try to find out details, not only about your achievements, knowledge and strong points but also about your shortcomings, inconsistencies and other traits from the 'dark side'. Your tasks before the interview are to discover your flaws and then to either improve your weak points and transform them into strengths or conceal them by emphasizing your strengths (an 'attack is the best defence' tactic).

Whenever your have to tell an interviewer about any mistakes you made (keep it to the minimum) quickly point out what you've learned from those lessons and stress that you never repeat your mistakes. That is the best way to neutralize the negative impact past mistakes may have.

Ideally, you should try the proper way: forcing yourself to change for better. To be successful in that approach two things are required: first, a lot of time and, second, determination, perseverance and hard, hard work. Most job applicants have neither.

Should you opt for a radical change of your shortcomings, start by visiting your local library and studying the numerous self-help and self-improvement books available or by enrolling on motivation and 'self-mastery' courses. Obstacles belong in the same category as weaknesses. Both are working against you. These are some of the significant hindrances that you should eliminate, neutralize or reduce.

## Inferiority complex

*I have no inferiority complex, and I'm not frightened by big sounding names. When I'm confronted by powerful people, I remind myself that all men use lavatory paper.*

Robert Maxwell

No additional words are really necessary here. In a nutshell, don't be afraid of anybody, don't overestimate anybody and don't be intimidated by anybody. Maintain your self-esteem and never lose belief in your abilities. Be constantly aware of your value. You can even inflate it a bit; just don't underestimate yourself and doubt your position.

## Balance of power

*The price of ability does not depend on merit, but on supply and demand.*

George Bernard Shaw, Socialism And Superior Brains, in *Fortnightly Review*, April 1894

Most job hunters feel that the employers dictate terms in the recession-hit job market, due to the increased competition for jobs and the plethora of high-calibre applicants who are prepared to work for peanuts. This is only partially true, however.

By using the right strategies, a planned and systematic approach to interviewing, and all the help at your disposal, you can greatly diminish the negative aspects of the tight job market. Employers *do* want the best applicants, and are usually prepared to stretch themselves to get them.

The majority (say 80%) of people that apply for the job you want will not pass the first, résumé, stage. They have no chance whatsoever. Of the other 20%, who are qualified and have the right experience, the short list will be created. Your first task is to be on that list. To achieve that you need a good résumé. The rest is covered in this book.

## Competitors

Never underestimate the quality and strength of your competitors. Always prepare yourself thoroughly for the interview. Explore all possibilities, especially everything that could go wrong, because there is a great chance that it will (Murphy's Law). Keep in mind that job hunting (especially interviewing) is pure Darwinism: only the fittest candidate will survive and get the job. However, to overestimate your competition would be an even worse sin. By doing that you automatically lower your self-esteem and your chances for success.

Be confident and composed. Don't compare yourself to others. Compete with yourself. Strive towards constant improvement of your skills and abilities, especially communication techniques and job interviewing skills.

*While competing for jobs, we all make mistakes. Your goal should be to make fewer mistakes than your opponents.*

## The eternal question of experience

When judging someone's experience employers seldom distinguish between a person with ten years of experience on various tasks and assignments and one with one year of relevant experience repeated ten times. If you belong to the first group and compete for a job with someone with longer but less diversified and relevant experience, point out this difference to the potential employer. It is quality that should matter, not quantity. Open their eyes if necessary, so they can see you better, in the best light.

Next time you come across a job advertisement that asks for more experience than you actually possess, don't be discouraged. Apply anyway. Present your case, convince them that your other qualities and the relevancy of your (shorter than required) experience will be far more beneficial to the employer than merely 'doing your time'.

# Improving your interviewing skills and performance

*'Then you shall judge yourself,' the king answered. 'That is the most difficult thing of all. It is much more difficult to judge oneself than to judge others. If you succeed in judging yourself rightly, then you are indeed a man of true wisdom.'*

Antoine De Saint-Exupery, *The Little Prince*

One thing job hunters have to understand is that their skills are commodities that are sought after by employers. Skills in the job market could be equated to other commodities on the stock market. Their values go up or down, depending on the supply and demand – i.e. how many people are buying or selling the shares (looking for a job) and at what price (how much money they are prepared to accept in return for their services).

Your ongoing task is to keep improving your skills and adding value to them. By skills I mean your professional knowledge and know-how as well as your job-hunting skills (résumé writing, interviewing, career planning). Your job-hunting skills are not valuable to employers, but they are extremely valuable to you, because they help you to promote your real abilities, knowledge and experience.

Interviewing skills are probably the most important in the whole process, and, unfortunately, the most difficult ones to master. The good news is that these skills are portable – you can apply them in any real-life situation and reap the benefits. We are not talking about God-given skills and abilities, we are talking about common sense: talking to other people, listening, interacting with them. We are talking about fundamental techniques in handling people.

In real life most of the time we don't see or feel the direct consequences of using (or not using) our people-handling skills. In the job interview things are more obvious. There are only two possible outcomes – you either get the job or you don't. It is much easier to measure your performance against known standards and expectations. The aim of this book is to explain and analyse the standards against which you will be evaluated, to advise you on the best tactics and on when and how to use them.

Our next step is to go through a few basic interviewing skills and the ways of improving them.

## Learn how to listen

Most people are not good listeners. They never listen to anyone for long. They talk mostly about themselves and interrupt others without waiting for them to finish talking. Even if they don't interrupt, they don't pay attention to what others are saying, because they are busy rehearsing what they are going to say next. This is probably worse than talking too much, for they are neither making nor hearing a point.

These are all cardinal sins in the job interview. You should listen very carefully, not only to what the interviewers are saying but also to how they are saying it. It is not enough to simply hear, you have to *listen* aggressively. Listening skills are amongst your most valuable possessions.

Remember:

- Do not jump to conclusions before the interviewer finishes a statement.
- Never interrupt the interviewer, even if you strongly disagree with him.
- Do not discard information you don't want to hear or don't like.
- Listen for main ideas, not for details.
- If the interviewer talks slowly, don't let your mind wander around. No daydreaming. Use that time to analyse what's being said and why, to anticipate, weigh the evidence, mentally rehearse the interviewer's points and listen 'between the lines' for clues.
- Don't tune out if the delivery is poor. Concentrate on content, not on errors in speech.
- Fight or avoid distractions. Concentrate.

## Be time-sensitive

The main problem in interviewing is time. The interviewer has to evaluate all aspects of the candidate in a strictly limited amount of time, say an hour or so. On the other hand, you have to convince the interviewer that you are the best person for the job and you have only one hour (or even less) to do so. Therefore, both you and the interviewer have to be time-sensitive.

Experienced interviewers know or feel how much time they can (or want to) spend on each particular question or area to be covered. You should know too, to the best of your abilities. The time control is usually in your hands, because answering questions takes much more time than asking them. You must constantly read the interviewer and make sure that you confine yourself within certain time limits.

Your answers should be neither too short nor too long. By giving very short answers you force the interviewer to ask you additional questions and the fluidity of the conversation is gone. There are too many pauses and the whole interview sounds like an interrogation. On the other hand, if your answers are too long, the interviewer may get all sorts of ideas:

- The candidate is not capable of distinguishing between important and unimportant information.
- He has got no respect for me and my time.

- She bores me immensely.
- This person has verbal diarrhoea and would not be able to keep secrets and confidential information. Therefore he could not be trusted.

Once the job interview starts, you must have a clear idea of how much time to devote to each answer and when to ask relevant questions. Of course, don't be rigid. Just remember the old cliché: 'time is money'. It's certainly true at the job interview.

## Improve your vocabulary

Your ability to communicate, especially verbally, is exceptionally important! Words are very powerful – used wisely, they will help you go a long way towards the top. If you are not careful and use the wrong words at the wrong time or in front of the wrong person, you could bring about your own downfall.

With words you relate to people and communicate your feelings and thoughts to them. Therefore, words are the best tool for influencing and controlling people!

Your vocabulary is you – it's your fingerprint. So, if you want to improve your image and your chances for success, make sure you continually expand your vocabulary. The research shows that only three to four thousand words separate people with large from those with small vocabularies.

*The way we say things is quite often more important than what we actually say!*

In contrast to learning the grammatical rules and the syntax of English language, vocabulary expanding can be fun. You can do it 'formally', by studying text books and encyclopedias, or 'informally', by jotting down every unknown word you encounter while reading a book, a magazine or even while watching television (however, television is generally not a highly intellectual medium, so it is doubtful that you will find many sophisticated words there).

Later, go through a good dictionary to find out the exact meaning of the words and try to remember the contexts in which they were used.

The vocabulary of an average person almost stops growing in their mid-twenties. Therefore, it is necessary to make extra effort and start building up your knowledge of words.

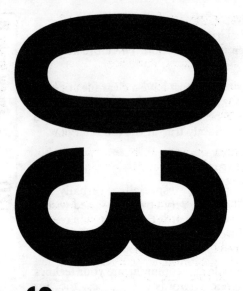

# 03

## selling yourself

In this chapter you will learn:
- tips on how to dress for an interview
- how to tallk about yourself
- how to evaluate the interviewer

# Your appearance: dress for the part

*Everyone lives by selling something.*
Robert Louis Stevenson

Job hunting is like a game: when you write your résumé and apply for a job, you're in the qualification rounds. Should you pass the qualifications you get a place in the final game: the job interview.

It isn't difficult to be a winner on a paper. But in real life the differences will stand out, and your looks and appearance contribute to those differences.

The authors of some self-improvement books I've read devoted ten or twenty pages to the ways of 'dressing for success'. With all due respect, I find this ridiculous. Individual styles are different, fashion changes every year or so, people in different countries dress differently, the positions you will be interviewed for will dictate different norms and standards, different employers place different values on the way you may dress.

Some common sense rules do exist, though. Let's take a look at them:

1 Always be clean and well groomed. Pay special attention to your hair, nails and teeth. They should be spotless!
2 Never wear too much jewellery, especially big rings, bracelets, cuff links or golden chains. Earrings for men are definitely not recommended.
3 Don't wear short-sleeved shirts at the interview. You don't want to look like some used car salesman or a campaigning politician (unless you *are* one!).
4 Never take off your suit jacket, unless you have to. The jacket gives you more authority.
5 Depending on the job you are applying for, carry a good briefcase, preferably black leather. It will enhance your image tremendously. This particularly applies to accountants, lawyers, engineers, managers and other professionals.
6 Always wear a watch. It will help you project a business image and discreetly tell the interviewer that your time is valuable. A word of caution here – don't look at the watch. This tells the interviewer that you are anxious to get out and that you aren't really interested in the job.

7 Men, wear an expensive-looking, silk tie of appropriate pattern. Because most men's suits look alike, a nice tie contributes to your image much more than you would expect. However, stick to conservative designs with a dash of originality. Bow-ties or Texan leather ties are definitely out (except for waiters and oil magnates).

*Dress so that you feel you look good.*

Never follow the trends if they don't suit you. Some 'consultants' say dress in black or dark blue only. That's nonsense. You might not look good in dark colours. Follow your own feelings or consult your spouse or a good friend. Unbiased advice is always welcome.

If you need a new outfit, invest your money wisely. Buy first class only. It will be money well spent. If you want to give a first-class performance, don't go in wearing second-class attire.

Have at least two different outfits, just in case something goes wrong. Besides, if you go for a second or third interview with the same employer you should change your clothes, otherwise you may project a picture of a typical job-beggar: one suit = timidity, lack of originality, stiffness, predictability.

Don't just keep your interview outfits in the wardrobe. Wear them when you go out to restaurants or the theatre. That will make you feel comfortable wearing them and help you to be relaxed and natural at the interview. The worst possible thing would be to go in to an interview wearing brand-new clothes in which you feel uncomfortable and unnatural.

# Talking about yourself: the bottom line

*Man is like a rabbit, you catch him by the ears.*

Blaise Pascal

Your purpose in a job interview is to convince the prospective employer that you are the most suitable candidate for the job.

*Your success in interviewing will be determined more by your ability to market and promote yourself than by your actual knowledge and work experience.*

In order to do that, you have to present yourself to the interviewers in the right way, tell them what you have done in the past and what you could do for them should they select you for the job. The bottom line is therefore a simple one. How to achieve it is another story.

Some people find talking about themselves difficult and feel uncomfortable while doing so. If you want to become a 'professional' interviewee (see last chapter), learn to talk about yourself in the most effective manner, without false modesty but without boasting.

There are eleven basic rules for your self-presentation. Study them carefully and constantly keep them in mind. The effort will pay off.

1 Say only good things about your previous employers.
2 Be future-oriented – or at least leave an impression that you are!
3 Select your words carefully.
4 Avoid asking inappropriate questions.
5 Listen carefully to what the interviewers say and frame your answers accordingly.
6 Some interviewers like to talk about themselves. Let them.
7 Develop and use your own style to deliver a perfect performance.
8 Never argue with the interviewers.
9 Always talk in the other person's terms.
10 Be prepared to talk about your mistakes and shortcomings.
11 Place a high value on yourself – don't be a 'job-beggar'.

Let's take a look at each point in turn.

## Say only good things about your previous employers

Even if your boss treated you unfairly, even if you didn't like your former place of work and people you worked with, keep it to yourself. Do not criticize, complain or accuse. Think of positive things to say about your former employers and remember to project sincerity, even when 'bending the truth', for you'll be bending it in your favour!

A personnel officer was interviewing applicants for a supervisory position on the shop floor.

After the initial interviews he selected the two best candidates for the final interview. After talking to the first man, the personnel officer had no further questions for the candidate. At the end of the interview, the candidate asked the following question: 'What could you tell me about the people who work here? What are the workers like?' The personnel man wasn't sure what to say and responded with a question: 'What were the people like at your last place of work?'

The applicant looked at the personnel officer and said: 'The company I just left had mainly pretty bad people. They were not friendly and I wasn't happy there. The management had no respect for workers and workers were difficult to supervise. They were just no good. That is why I want to join your company.'

The interviewer looked directly at the candidate and said: 'Well, I'm afraid that most people we employ here are of the same kind. Things you are looking for are not easy to find.'

After interviewing the second candidate and answering similar questions about the job itself and the company's plans for the future, the personnel officer said to the interviewee: 'Tell me something about the people you used to work with and the workers you used to supervise.'

'The people at my former place of work were really nice and friendly. I haven't had any problems supervising the shop floor. I enjoyed the time I spent with them, but due to the limited opportunities there for myself and my family I am looking for a position with the company like yours. It was not easy to leave, but we had no choice.'

'Well, you are in luck, young man', the interviewer said, 'because that's exactly the kind of people that work for this company. You'll really like them and they'll like you. Welcome aboard!'

We find exactly what we seek.

## Be future-oriented – or at least leave an impression that you are

Most applicants think that prospective employers are interested in their past. They are, but only because they believe that by analysing the candidate's past they can predict their future behaviour and performance on the job.

Whatever you say about your education and past experience, say it in such a way as to convince the interviewers that:

- You were in control of the events.
- You achieved something.
- You can do the same good job for them.

By being a future-oriented person you project a sense of purpose and direction. Employers like that attitude and place a high value on it.

## Select your words carefully

In order to create an image of competency, efficiency and integrity in the interviewer's eyes, use words that are easy to understand, short and expressive, words that generate the right mental pictures and are appropriate. By using inappropriate or confusing words you may make the interviewer think that:

- You are boring and dull.
- You are full of yourself and will have difficulty in working with others.
- You don't really understand what you are talking about.
- You talk in terms that are too general and cannot give examples and real-life situations.

The bottom line in choosing the words is to keep the interviewer's attention!

## Avoid asking inappropriate questions

Victor Kiam, one of the most successful entrepreneurs, in his book *Going For It!* tells the following story:

> *If you are in position where you are trying to secure a position, you certainly don't want the company to think you are already dreaming about retirement. Not too long ago, a young man ended an interview by asking me what Remington's pension plan was. He was about 25 years old! I answered him, 'Son, you'll never find out'.*

Always keep in mind that just one clumsy question may set you back or even get you out of the game completely. If unsure about the impact that the question you intend to ask will have on the interviewer, don't ask it. But, if there is nothing to lose and a lot to gain, go for it. The real challenge is to assess the current situation and make that decision in a matter of seconds.

This is where interviewing experience and know-how come into the equation. But as interviewing is not mathematics, my advice to you would be to rely on your own 'gut feelings'.

## Listen carefully to what the interviewers say and frame your answers accordingly

Say, for example, the interviewer tells you at the beginning of the interview that the position requires someone energetic, hard working and committed. Further down the line you should use this priceless information to frame your answers.

For example, if asked 'What were the reasons for your success on that project?' you may answer: 'I worked long hours and committed myself to the project. It required lots of energy, but I always give a hundred per cent.' The interviewer will think: 'This is the type of person I want for this job.' This type of feedback will prove the most useful in interviewing.

## Some interviewers like to talk about themselves. Let them

A few years ago I was interviewed for an engineering position with one of Australia's largest companies. The Chief Engineer was a friendly guy, I felt at ease with him and the interview went well. It was probably the easiest one in my whole career! Why? Because the interviewer talked all the time. I hardly spoke.

He explained the job to me, the company's history and plans, career opportunities and so on. Did I interrupt him? You can bet I didn't. After about an hour or so in his office we parted on very friendly terms. A week after that I was invited again to his office where he introduced me to my future boss. The same scenario went on. I was offered a job with almost no effort. God certainly works in mysterious ways.

## Develop and use your own style to deliver a perfect performance

*The style is the man.*
Robert Frost

It isn't easy to define style, but people remember style as much as substance. In the job game, style should be recognized as an important factor in dramatizing your ideas, getting your message across to the interviewers and making the right impression.

Style is closely related to your personality and your socioeconomic class. Style can be observed through the way you walk, talk, through your vocabulary, your sense of humour, your manners, clothes, your smile and gestures.

It is not easy to change your style; however, it is not impossible. It takes practice and self-control. There are quite a few self-improvement books that deal with those improvements. Study them. There is nothing to lose, and a lot to gain. The rest is up to you.

## Never argue with the interviewers

*Keep your ego from ruining your chances of success: never argue or question the interviewer's views!*

I remember some of my colleagues in college, not because we were friends or because they were smart, but because they used to argue with the lecturers and professors, who in turn (for obvious reasons) did not like those students very much. They passed their exams, but with much greater difficulties than the rest of us. The other side used every opportunity for vindication.

There is no retaliation of this kind in interviewing, but you can be sure that you won't get the job. Period. By strongly expressing your views and criticizing or questioning the interviewer you may exhilarate your spirit and feel good for a moment, but you are going to lose in the long run.

## Always talk in the other person's terms

Each one of us could talk about ourselves for hours and hours, because we are our own favourite subject. But the interviewers are not interested in you directly, all they want to know is:

• Are you qualified to do the job?
• Can you do the job?
• Will you do the job?

So, the purpose of the interview is to say as much as possible about yourself in an organized and logical manner, convincing the person across the table that you can do the job better than other candidates. To get your message across always try to establish what it is that the interviewer wants – what sort of person he or she would like to see on that job, what traits they like or dislike in people, what factors they consider important in successful performance on the job and so on.

***Always talk in terms of the interviewer's interests.***

The principle above applies to any kind of human relations, not just to job interviews. Here is a little story that I would like you to remember whenever you talk to other people:

---

An older woman and her nephew went to buy her a car. The first car salesman asked the woman: 'What type of car do you have in mind, madam?'

'Oh, I want a car that can take me to the library a few times a week', she replied.

'Any of these cars can take you to the library.' the salesman answered. They had a look around, but left without buying a car.

In the second dealership she was asked a similar question.

'I need a car which I can drive to the library a few times a week.'

'This is completely irrelevant', the salesman said, 'you should be concerned about space, economy, quality and spare parts and service.' They again looked around, but didn't find anything of interest.

In the third dealership the woman said: 'I need a car that can take me to the library'.

'I see,' said the sales manager, 'I believe you are looking for a short-distance car for daytime driving?'

'That's exactly what I'm looking for,' she replied.

'Sounds like you need a small, compact car that's very easy to park and drive.'

'Spot on,' said the woman.

'I'm not sure we have got anything like that,' the manager said, 'but I'll check right now.'

After five minutes, he returned with a smile: 'We have a car for you, madam. Would you like to test drive it?'

The woman drove the car around the block and fifteen minutes later, after signing the papers, happily drove away to the library.

## Be prepared to talk about your mistakes and shortcomings

*To err is human. To forgive is not company policy.*
Anonymous sign to company executives

For quite a long time I was convinced that employers wanted to know only about my achievements, capabilities and successfully accomplished tasks. When you have only a limited amount of time to impress the interviewers, it is normal to give it your best shot and tell them about your strengths and all nice things you could do for them. The truth, however, was slightly different. They also wanted to know about the other side of the coin – they were interested in the mistakes I made, the tasks and projects I could have done better, the areas I wanted to improve in.

So, when asked about some of the mistakes you made, you must select the least detrimental information and present it to them in such a way that the outcomes say something positive about you. Interviewers should be left with an impression that you are not repeating mistakes and that you give your best in every situation, especially when dealing with people.

The biggest mistake you can make in the interview is to imply that you have never made a mistake. Why is that so?

Employers want to hire people who've had their wins and losses. That experience gives those candidates the strength and knowledge of how to capitalize on losses and the ability to do a better job the next time by not repeating mistakes.

A person who has never made mistakes and hasn't had to overcome barriers will fall on their face when they hit the first obstacle. Employers don't like to pay for your mistakes and are not prepared to finance your 'education'. They prefer people whose former employers paid for the mistakes they made.

If you appear to openly discuss the events that went wrong when you made a mistake or were not able to do things properly, the interviewer will be much more inclined to believe you about your accomplishments and other good points. It will help you to establish confidentiality and trust and reinforce your credibility. However, don't be a straight shooter and tell them nothing but the truth: truth is a very relative term and should be treated as such. *Never* volunteer any information that makes you look stupid, careless, incompetent or inexperienced. Honesty creates trust, not suspicion.

## Place a high value on yourself – don't be a 'job-beggar'

*Always make yourself essential, that's been my golden rule.*

Sir Joh Bjelke-Petersen

The biggest mistakes I made in my early days of job hunting were:

- Approaching employers as a 'beggar' not a 'chooser'. I waited for the companies to select me and offer me a job, instead of choosing the company I wanted to work for. I left to chance most of the things I could have had control over.
- I was too timid and complacent in the whole process. I just accepted the terms, without negotiating for even one second. I accepted the salary, the benefits, the job description, etc. I even took jobs without seeing the towns I was going to live in, without visiting my future place of work, without talking to my new colleagues. And guess what? I made the same mistake twice. Shame on me.
- When offered a job I felt that the employers were doing me a big favour. I didn't think about my assets such as knowledge, skills and my personality. I didn't regard them as valuable commodities that the employers would benefit from. Somehow I forgot five years of hard study, sixteen years of schooling and all my past efforts. I sowed, but I didn't reap.
- I was selling my abilities short. I had a self-destructive tendency to exaggerate other people's intelligence and skills while underestimating my own. Not only that: I didn't believe in my success. I was a sceptic.

My advice is to do the opposite of everything I did. Believe me, it will spare you disappointment, frustration and self-hatred. Never accept what's offered to you initially. Negotiate. Name your terms. Make them work hard to get you. You'll probably catch them unprepared, because too many people are beggars, not choosers. By placing a high value on yourself you automatically change your status in the employer's eyes.

*Play hard to get and (later) hard to keep.*

## The delivery

Albert Mehrabian, American psychologist, tried to measure the relative importance of the three basic communication channels

– the content, tone of voice and body language (gestures, posture, facial expressions). His research revealed that the actual content, or the words used to convey a message contributed only around 10 per cent to the overall impact, compared with almost 40 per cent from the tone of voice and more than 50 per cent from the body language!

It sounds illogical and hard to believe, but we have to realize that most of our thoughts and actions are based on feelings and impressions, not on logic, no matter how hard we try to project the image of systematic, no-nonsense thinkers. Every interviewer probably tries to be objective and neutral but, at the end, his or her overall impression of you will either get you that job or leave you unemployed. So, whatever you say, make sure that your tone of voice and your body language are reinforcing your message, not contradicting its content; otherwise, your message won't get through to the interviewer. Keep the following proportions always in your mind:

- words (message content): 10 per cent of impact
- tone of voice: 40 per cent of impact
- body language: 50 per cent of impact.

## The importance of silence

Silence in a job interview can be either your powerful ally or your worst enemy. When you talk to the interviewer or answer questions, use pauses to emphasize your point and to build up eager anticipation for what you are going to say next. Those periods of silence will give you an opportunity to make eye contact with the interviewer and study their reactions to what you've just said. Don't hesitate to use silence. Speak in a slow, relaxed manner. Pause every now and then to grab the interviewer's attention.

Some interviewers use silence as a tool for eliciting further response from a candidate. Once you have said what you wanted to say, they will leave you 'in limbo' for a few very long seconds. You must resist the urge to say something just to break the silence. Usually that 'something' is some information you don't want the interviewer to know. And that's exactly their reason for using this common tactic.

Think about it as a game of tennis. You've returned the serve and the ball is in your opponent's court. All you have to do is wait patiently.

# Evaluating the interviewer

If you do your research properly, by the time you enter the interview you should know some basic things about the interviewer – name, position and possibly some details of their work history, achievements and personality. These details should be the basis for your analysis. You have to predict what kind of person the interviewer is, what he or she is looking for in an applicant, etc. However, in most cases it's almost impossible to get this type of information beforehand. Therefore, you have to do that evaluation during the interview. The sooner you get the crucial information the better, for it can help you to frame your answers and 'fine tune' your performance during the later stage of the interview.

The tactic to remember here is '**AAA**'.

1 **Anticipate** the interviewer's questions, reactions, attitudes, fears, problems.
2 **Adapt** to the interviewer's style, manners, views, attitude. Try to share their values and get into their line of thinking.
3 **Act** upon the feedback from the interviewer. Use the clues he or she will be giving you to your advantage. If the interviewer is inclined towards, say, capital accounting, place the emphasis on that aspect of your accounting experience.

Another major objective of evaluating and monitoring the interviewer is to constantly keep track of how well you are doing so that you can recognize negative developments as early as possible. That way you can reverse them in your favour and pick up the indicators of positive feedback in order to further reinforce the good impressions.

## The interviewer's body language and behaviour

As the interviewer evaluates your looks and body language, you have to play the same game in order to get some feedback on how you're doing. So, let's take a look at the basic grammar rules of an interviewer's body language and their meanings.

A word of caution here: body language is based on preconceptions and stereotypes. The same behaviour in different situations could have different meanings and therefore can mislead you into false conclusions. The explanations below are only the most common interpretations.

## Inclination and posture
- Leaning towards the applicant: sign of interest, involvement, positive intentions – *good sign*.
- Sitting erect – *neutrality*.
- Leaning back: sign of detachment or superiority. He or she may be evaluating the applicant or could simply be relaxed – *mixed signal*.
- Rigid posture: probably caused by some negative or defensive response to something you said – *bad sign*.
- Slumping may signal indifference, fatigue or rejection – *beware*.

## Openness
- Arms crossed at the chest: closed or defensive attitude – *beware*.
- Clenched fists: aggressiveness, closed attitude – *bad sign*.
- Smile accompanied with an occasional nod: approval of what you are saying – *good sign*.
- Interviewer's body not facing you directly: emotional detachment or thinking about some other business – *bad sign*.

## Small signs that mean big problems
- The arm supporting the head: *boredom*.
- Drumming the fingers on the table – *impatience* and *irritation*.
- Tapping of the feet on the floor – *impatience* and *irritation*.
- Glancing at the watch – *impatience* – the end of the interview is imminent.

One common tendency amongst applicants when they are interviewed by a relaxed, friendly interviewer is to adopt or imitate (usually unconsciously) the interviewer's behaviour. I wouldn't recommend it. Relax and behave naturally, but always maintain a professional and formal attitude. What is appropriate for the interviewer may not be (and usually isn't) acceptable behaviour for the applicant.

# Recognize the interviewer's problems

During your job hunt you'll meet different types of interviewers. Some will be personnel managers, personnel officers or professional recruitment consultants, who can be called professional interviewers. However, there is another group you are likely to meet: managers, supervisors, chief engineers, team leaders or professionals in various disciplines – but not in recruitment.

For some of the people in the second group interviewing may not be the easiest of tasks. Some will feel uneasy because they don't have much experience in interviewing. They might run out of questions to ask or could have to consult the company's procedures and policies book constantly, in order to follow the prescribed format and ask every candidate the same set of questions.

Some interviewers rely on your résumé as a backbone for the conversation and some talk too much because they don't know what questions to ask or how to interpret them, so they rely mostly on 'gut feeling'.

Despite differences in background and in personal interviewing style and techniques, there is one fear common amongst interviewers: making the mistake of hiring the wrong person. Should they select you for the job and you, for whatever reason, do not perform on the job or leave for greener pastures after only a few months, they would find it very difficult to face their boss and justify their selection. It would make them look incompetent and not very thorough in their selection procedures. That is why your every gesture, every answer and every question has to convey the same message: 'I'm the right person for the job, I can make you look good in your boss's eyes and I'm here to stay.' Remember that.

Always try to make the interviewer comfortable and establish a cordial contact. Show your friendly side. Avoid long pauses and aggressive or pushy questions, statements or gestures. Make the interviewers feel your respect for them and show your appreciation for the opportunity to talk to them.

## Basic interviewer personalities and how to treat them

> *Knowing something about the interviewer is as important as knowing everything about yourself.*

In order to use the right strategy in your dealings with a particular interviewer, you have to quickly form an opinion about that person. You have only two to three minutes for an initial analysis. This is the time it takes to establish an initial contact and start a 'question and answer' session. Look for the clues:

- **The surroundings:** office, decor, furniture, books, pictures on the walls, trophies, awards, quotations on the walls, photographs on the table, writings on the whiteboard, etc.
- **The interviewer:** appearance, age, body posture, clothes, accent, facial expressions …

Most interviewers could be classified into basic personality types. However, interbreeds are more common. Here are the characteristics of the main groups.

### The professional

The professional is an experienced interviewer, who comes out of the office to greet you in a pleasant and friendly manner. Once in the office, he or she makes you feel relaxed and comfortable. For the first minute or two he talks about traffic jams, the weather, your problems in finding the place or any other 'small' topic, just to break the ice.

He or she will ask only relevant questions, avoiding trick questions and interrogatory style, and maintaining an attitude of respect and understanding. The questions are formulated in a precise and concise way, using simple language. He or she knows what to find out about you and usually accomplishes this without you figuring out subtle moves and tactics. This type of interviewer is very hard to manipulate, but they are also human and some emotions will show, giving you valuable clues.

- **Tactics:** This is what all interviewers should look and act like. I haven't met too many, but there are some around. It's more likely that you'll meet them in personnel departments of big or progressive companies.

### The interrogator

This person probably watched too many 'Gestapo' movies in their younger days. He or she tends to fire a series of quick and short questions at the candidate and expects an immediate response: doing that tests the applicant's behaviour in stressful situations and saves time in the process. This interviewer probably doesn't enjoy interviewing and isn't genuinely interested in job candidates.

It is very likely that you'll be facing a sunny window or a brightly lit lamp (just to test your nerves). You may be even kept waiting longer than usual outside the office, for the same purpose.

- **Tactics:** be optimistic and positive, and sound that way. Think of yourself as a professional actor in front of a hostile and unreceptive audience. Be a real professional. Don't take any short cuts: take your time and answer the questions the way you practised. Don't allow the interviewer to hurry you or make you feel uncomfortable. Ask lots of questions whenever your can. Attack is the best defence.

## The formalist

Spontaneity is not in this person's vocabulary. He or she follows the interview evaluation sheet as if it were The Bible, reads the questions in a monotonous and mechanical fashion and very seldom deviates from the script.

That rigid atmosphere puts most candidates off; they often feel tense and tend to adopt the interviewer's behavioural style and produce short and dull answers, which can only be to their disadvantage. Do not fall into that trap. Relax and perform your 'play' properly. Take your time to answer and do not rush.

- **Tactics:** Do not pay too much attention to that inflexible behaviour. Just try to be friendly and fire your shots as you practised them. Don't be intimidated by long pauses. Once you have said what you wanted to say, wait for the interviewer to say something. Don't volunteer any unnecessary information.

## The psychologist

This interviewer is probably a failed medical student who is pretending that he or she holds a degree in psychology. Such people use quasi-psychological methods in their 'analysis', usually paying more attention to your non-verbal response than to what you actually say. Questions will be slightly different from the standard ones, perhaps about your parents, your childhood, your purpose in life, etc. You'll probably be asked some of the less common questions in Chapter 6 by this interviewer. You will recognize this type: they sound pretentious and constantly try to show off their ego.

- **Tactics:** Stay composed and ask for further clarification if you don't understand the question or if it's too broad. The interviewer will welcome the chance to further elaborate on their nebulous questions.

## The smooth talker

The 'silky' is the organization's man. He is here to lure you into the magic world of his firm. As an interviewer, he'll probably make a good impression on you, because he won't ask too many hard questions. That's his job. This type thrives in particular industries, especially where high staff turnover or shortages of labour are a constant problem.

- **Tactics:** Treat this person as a salesman. If the deal promised sounds too good to be true, it probably is. If you accept an offer, get everything in writing. But, before that, dictate your terms to test his flexibility and advance your bargaining position.

## The disorganized type

The office is generally in a mess. In some cases the interviewer may even be late for the interview. Enormous quantities of paper are piled up on the desk, which makes it difficult to even find your application. This person has difficulty in organizing his or her thoughts, especially if the conversation is frequently interrupted by phone calls.

In this case, there is an opportunity for you to take the interview into your control, naturally, without letting the interviewer realize. If you feel frustrated and think that this disorganized interview format may prove disadvantageous to you, suggest rescheduling the meeting for a time that will be more convenient to the interviewer. He or she will appreciate your concern, which will win a few important points on the interview sheet.

- **Tactics:** The disorganized type is usually friendly and flexible, which gives you a chance to present yourself in a proper manner, if you can handle the messy atmosphere.

## The pretentious type

This person's nose is kept high in the air. He likes interviewing because he gets somebody's undivided attention for an hour or so. He often speaks more than other types of interviewers, using complex words, and tends to ask complicated questions to test your knowledge. He usually tries to keep his distance, so don't expect too much friendliness. It is very likely that he suffers from some complex. Your task is to discover what that complex is and to frame your answers and behaviour accordingly.

The good old 'humble' approach is probably the best strategy here. Resist adopting this interviewer's style. For some strange reason, most people are very sensitive to flaws they possess themselves!

- **Tactics:** Don't be intimidated by this person's apparent knowledge and 'advanced' interviewing methods. Know your lines, but don't pretend that you know everything, otherwise you may become like him.

### The parent
The parent is usually a woman in her late forties or fifties, but there are some male specimens around. She is often very friendly and approachable. Her parental instincts make her adopt a specific way of treating younger applicants, who will be pampered, counselled and advised on every possible matter, if only they give her an opportunity to display her maternal qualities.

- **Tactics:** Although this type is not particularly dangerous, you have to be composed and project maturity and apparent confidentiality. Because of her personality, she tends to elicit confidential information from naive applicants very easily. She wants you to trust her and take your mask off. Your task is to make her believe she succeeded. That's what *apparent confidentiality* means. Stick to your lines, just say them in such a way that will make her think you are the most honest kid on the block.

## Interviewers' weaknesses and inconsistencies

*In a hierarchy every employee tends to rise to his level of incompetence.*

Laurence J. Peter

This observation is certainly true for some interviewers. They have no training in interviewing and recruiting techniques, yet they have to recruit staff. A recipe for disaster. Being amateurs in the process themselves, their main concern in most cases is to avoid making mistakes in hiring. The direct costs of those mistakes can be huge. That is the reason most interviewers are very cautious these days. Most of them know what type of person they want and what sort of answers they want to hear.

Your role, as a candidate or interviewee, is to reassure them that:

- You can and will do a good job for them.
- You will make them look good in their boss's eyes.
- You will justify their decision to hire you by your performance and achievements on the job.

## Factors that affect the outcome

The validity and the outcome of a job interview can be affected by a wide range of factors, most of which are due to the highly subjective nature of the interviewing process. The main factors are:

- First impressions count. Interviewers tend to make up their minds about candidates very early in the interview process. The order in which they receive information has an impact on their decisions.
- All applicants affect the interviewer's impression of subsequent candidates.
- Physical looks influence the outcome. Physically attractive candidates have better chances of getting jobs than unattractive ones.
- Negative information will receive more of the interviewer's attention than positive. Most interviewers use the negatives to screen applicants, turning the interview into a series of 'knockout' questions.
- Different interviewers place different value on the same information. Some emphasize communication skills, some work experience, some academic results, etc.
- Insufficient knowledge of the position and inexperience in interviewing may result in overlooking some important factors and overemphasizing the unimportant ones.

## The clonal effect

*First-rate people hire first-rate people; second-rate people hire third-rate people.*

Leo Rosten

Every time employers want to hire someone, they consider two basic things: the candidate's competency and ability to do the job; the fit between the individual and the organization. Employers ask themselves: will the candidate fit into the existing structure and become a productive member of the work force? In the process of doing that, they compare candidates with:

• themselves
• former employees in the same job
• prevalent stereotypes and preconceptions for the particular position.

The clonal effect is the tendency among managers and recruiters to hire people they understand, trust, feel comfortable with and who are the most predictable – in short, people like themselves. They are looking for people they have a fair chance of getting along with, who communicate well and share values. They try to multiply themselves by hiring candidates with similar backgrounds, from the same part of the country, of the same gender and age group.

You have probably noticed that most car salesmen look alike, behave in a very similar manner, use the same vocabulary, have the same values. Move to the next group – say, lawyers – and you see clones again: black suits, black leather briefcases, white shirts, complex choice of words, a tendency to argue about everything with everybody, etc. The list goes on and on.

The clonal effect makes it very difficult for certain job hunters to get hired. Immigrants, minorities, women, people from different backgrounds. The best they can do is try to emulate the perceived stereotypes for the job.

## Stereotypes

Stereotypes are preconceived, questionable ideas, views and opinions about other people – their origin, race, age, gender, background, physical looks, habits, marital status or any other trait.

They are frequently used by suspense and romance novelists and job interviewers. Stereotypes can work for you and against you. Unfortunately, there is nothing much you can do about most of them, like your race, sex, background and body shape. However, you *can* modify and neutralize others.

Neutralizing stereotypes is easily done through proper design of your résumé. *Never* write your weight, height, religion, number of children, type of car and other similarly irrelevant details on your résumé. Although most people include data such as age, marital status and nationality, you can omit it without hesitation.

Some typical stereotypes that may affect you in a hiring process:

- Tall and skinny people are nervous and impatient.
- Fat people are lazy. Sloppy body means sloppy mind.
- People who don't drink are a bit strange.
- Women are too emotional and therefore unpredictable.
- People with beards are introverts and misfits.
- Unemployed people would accept any job.
- People who change jobs frequently will continue to do so.
- Single people tend to change jobs more often. They are less stable and highly mobile, therefore cannot be expected to stay with the same employer for too long.
- People with accents cannot be trusted.

## The halo effect

In the selection process employers interview more than one candidate. The number can range from two to twenty, or even more. At the end of that process it is impossible for the interviewers to remember all candidates clearly. The fact (substantiated by research statistics) is that the candidates interviewed later in the process have a much better chance of getting a job.

*The last person interviewed has a distinct advantage, because the interviewer will remember him or her more clearly.*

Targeted selection interviews try to avoid this problem by forcing the interviewers to write their answers in a predefined format, in spaces provided on the interview sheets. Still, it isn't possible to eliminate this inconsistency. To forget is a natural human tendency. This is one of the reasons why the 'thank you' note after the interview is so important. It reminds the interviewer of you. Refer to Chapter 8 for more details.

You can usually arrange an interview for a later date. Don't be in 'the first bunch'. If you can, try to be amongst the last candidates interviewed. That can sometimes give you an distinct edge over your competitors.

# Inexperience – being conned by a professional interviewee

The first axiom of competency:

> *The potential for a competent interviewee to manage and manipulate an incompetent interviewer is far greater than for an incompetent interviewer to manage a competent interviewee.*

Professional interviewees know how to present themselves as model employees. They understand the qualities that are attractive to employers and frame their interview performances accordingly. For you, this book is the best starting point towards achieving the goal of becoming 'one of them'. For me, this book is a ticket to interviewers' black lists. But, that's life.

'The professionals' often manage to secure jobs for which they 'just' qualify. They leave other, much more qualified and competent, opponents far behind, because they realize the most important fact in interviewing:

> *People who can talk well about themselves, their experience, education and achievements, who can project (I didn't say possess) integrity, sincerity and the real interest in employers, are the ones who get jobs. The other, often more educated, more hard working, smarter or more experienced candidates who do not know how to sell themselves, don't get what they deserve – the best jobs! What an irony!*

A common perception amongst some inexperienced interviewers and most candidates is that job interviews should be formal 'question and answer' sessions, with interviewers controlling the situation at all times. Job interviews should be more than that – a mutual assessment and open exchange of information. A resemblance to a tennis match is apparent – candidates should take the initiative and gain some control over the interview, otherwise they would constantly be at the receiving end, trying to return the interviewer's serves. Professional interviewees successfully use this tactic. Interviews are very elusive and deceitful encounters. Both parties are selling hard. Interviewers often promote rotten, dull jobs with no future or advancement opportunities as 'first-class deals'. You have similar rights in selling yourself.

## The loneliness and boredom effects

'I have been having some trouble with a flower,' said the
little prince.
'Ah!' said the snake.
And they were both silent.
'Where are the men?' the little prince at last took up the
conversation again.
'It is a little lonely in the desert ...'
'It is also lonely among men,' the snake said.

Antoine De Saint-Exupery, *The Little Prince*

In a typical corporate hierarchy, relationships are usually rigidly
defined. Each person is your boss (superior), your colleague or
your subordinate (somebody who reports to you and is
supervised by you). Such rigidly defined relationships are far
from conducive to friendship and intimacy, yet friendship and
human face is what many employers long for in a dull, sterile
and often hostile corporate world. People are afraid of opening
up, of admitting their fears, concerns, errors and other feelings
which have no place in an orthodox business environment. The
same applies to interviewers. Some are lonely, some frustrated,
some in a need of a sympathetic ear. If you can make them feel
relaxed, appreciated and respected, you will score some
crucially important points!

Most individual interviewers will prefer a friendly and likeable
person – even one less qualified and experienced – to someone
who appears stern and cold. The message: smile, be genuinely
interested in the interviewer and the firm and watch your
chances of getting a job rocket.

## Emphasize your 'hands-on' experience and practical attitude

Each interviewer constantly sends signals to prospective
employees about the things their company values the most. One
very common conception is that practicality, hands-on
involvement and participation in daily activities are more
valuable than sitting behind one's desk and shuffling papers and
devising policies. 'Hard hat' companies promote leadership
through actions and results instead of words.

What message should you be sending to these interviewers? That you don't rely unduly on your competence, status or experience; you like to be where the action is, with your sleeves rolled up, mastering the tasks, learning things that those you manage have to learn. Your strengths are improvisation, breaking the barriers between 'us' and 'them', delivering decisive blows to bureaucracy and the artificial division between intellectual and physical labour.

# 04

## interview formats and evaluation methods

**In this chapter you will learn:**
- about different types of interviews
- about the ways in which you will be evaluated
- how to approach psychological and aptitude tests

# Screening interviews

Employers use screening interviews to determine whether the candidate has sufficient basic qualifications and experience to warrant a formal interview. Usually they are not targeted to a specific job and are used to streamline walk-in candidates. Normally, this type of interview is conducted by one interviewer and the duration is generally limited to 15–30 minutes.

In the current economic climate, characterized by high unemployment, screening interviews are quickly regaining their importance. In times of high employment screening interviews are a less common form of pre-selection. In some industries, and for some vocations, screening interviews are an essential part of the selection process.

# Campus recruiting interviews

Interviews conducted by campus recruiters could be classified as a special form of screening interviews. Instead of the applicants coming to the company, the company sends a recruiter, usually a personnel officer, to interview them. This is not an easy job, due to the need to interview so many applicants in a relatively short time.

The recruiter gives basic information about the organization, its operations and goals, and specific positions that are available for young graduates, including details on the length and structure of company's graduate training programmes.

# Telephone interviews

Telephone interviews mostly serve as screening interviews. I have had only two telephone interviews in my career. The first one was with a large government organization in Sydney. There were three interviewers on the other side of the line and each one of them asked me one or two questions. The whole conversation lasted about 15 minutes. Believe it or not, I was offered a job in Sydney, but I didn't take it. I don't like big cities and it was too easy to be true. Something wasn't quite right.

The second one took place recently. It was just like any one-on-one interview – I had to answer 20 or so questions, the man on the other end of the line was (judging by pauses after each of my answers) taking notes and the whole session lasted more than an hour. The company involved is in the oil and gas business, so he wasn't worried about the phone bill. I didn't get the job, probably because I couldn't use my charm and other selling techniques over the phone.

If you ever get a job over the phone, there are only two reasons:

1 The employer is in a hurry to fill the vacancy by employing (almost) anybody, in which case you should ask yourself why was that the case. Would you take a job that nobody else wanted?
2 You've mastered your interviewing skills and become a real professional in selling yourself over the phone. Congratulations!

In either case, beware. If you were an employer, investing, say, £30,000 in a new employee (one year's salary and benefits), wouldn't you like to at least meet your future employee before offering him or her a job?

If possible, avoid telephone interviews. For something this important, you need face-to-face communication. If the employer is genuinely interested in you, they should invite you for a proper interview and pay your necessary travel expenses.

# Group interviews

Group interviews are not common, but some companies use them to evaluate a number of candidates at the same time. There are usually two or more interviewers: it isn't easy for one person to properly evaluate five or more applicants at the same time. This interview format makes it easier for the employer to compare the applicants and determine the ones that project themselves best in a competitive atmosphere.

Group interviews are designed to intimidate candidates and evaluate them under awkward and stressful conditions. Here are a few points to remember if you want to leave a good impression in these interviews:

• Stay composed and maintain your poise.
• Learn from other candidates' responses – you'll have more time to evaluate the interviewer and your competitors while they answer questions, and use that knowledge in formulating your answers.

- Don't criticize your opponents' answers, attitudes and opinions.
- Don't be intimidated by the situation.

## Panel interviews

The panel interview is probably the most common evaluation method used by employers (especially the big organizations) when recruiting professional and managerial personnel. By using a panel of three or four interviewers, they try to establish an unbiased and objective picture of a candidate.

The interviewers usually come from different departments or sections of the company. One of them will lead the group and frame the whole session. Almost without exception, that person will be the personnel officer, personnel manager or somebody with similar title, for they regard themselves best qualified to 'hire and fire'. Other members of the panel will include the immediate supervisor or manager, who hires the candidate to work in his or her section, the department manager and, in some cases (if needed), a specialist whose task is to evaluate the candidate's specialist knowledge.

This type of interview tends to be highly structured. Each member of the panel evaluates a specific area of the candidate's background, and by doing that the employers are assured that all important points, such as the candidate's experience, qualifications and personality, will be explored and evaluated.

When asked a question by one of the interviewers, devote more attention to that person, but maintain eye contact with the other members of the panel while answering the question. Generally try to divide your attention equally between them. Don't speak to the leader only or the person who asked a question. Try to remember the names and who is who in the organization. Frame your answers accordingly and modify your approach. If you talk to an accountant, try to think like him, when you talk to an engineer, talk in her (technical) terms.

## One-on-one interviews

In this case only one person evaluates the candidates and decides who to hire for the job, either alone or after consultation with upper management. Although there are always some exceptions, this interview format is mostly used by smaller companies and when hiring non-professional personnel (secretaries, tradesmen, so-called 'blue-collar workers', etc.).

In most of these cases the qualifications and skills of the candidates are more clearly defined and easier to measure than those of professional employees (engineers, lawyers, scientists, accountants).

The interviewer is most likely to be the immediate supervisor or a manager to whom this position reports. The interview will be the best opportunity for both parties to evaluate each other.

# Lunch interviews

Every time you have an interview away from your home town, the interviewer will probably take you out for lunch, sometimes before, but usually after the actual interview. In most cases a quick tour will be organized around the company's premises and the 'official' interview would take place. After lunch, there might be some time left for another tour around the company, in order to meet other managers and employees, and perhaps a short sightseeing trip around town, for candidates to get a feeling about the place. The scenarios will vary from case to case, but there are some common rules to observe:

1 Always keep in mind that the other person will keep evaluating you, no matter where you go or what you do.
2 At lunch, follow basic common sense:
   - Eat where the interviewer wishes. Let him or her choose the place.
   - Stay away from alcohol, even if the interviewer orders wine or beer. You'll need a clear mind to present yourself in the right way. You may want to have a drink so as not to appear unsociable, but don't drink all of it. Even one drink could impair your judgement.
   - Choose a meal that is easy to eat, is not messy and does not leave foul breath.
   - Never order the most expensive item on the menu. Your choice should be in the same price range as the interviewer's meal. You might ask the interviewer to recommend something.
   - Let the interviewer pay for the meal. It's part of the recruiting expenses and nobody expects you to honour the bill. Do not offer to buy drinks or coffee.

2 Maintain your pose and don't become too friendly with the interviewers. Do not disclose too much and do not talk too much, or you will be left with a half-full plate while others are already ordering coffee. Make sure you ask a few job-related questions to slow the interviewer(s) down.

## Situational interviews

Some employers go beyond the conventional interviewing techniques and try to evaluate the applicants' skills through situational evaluation. Behavioural simulations and job replica tests are sometimes used for that purpose.

Behavioural simulations are used to test the applicants in certain areas which are difficult to evaluate through normal 'question and answer' sessions. They can take various forms, such as sales presentations for the evaluation of sales people, interview simulations for people that will be dealing with customers or clients, scheduling exercises for people in project control, purchasing, logistics, etc.

The job replica tests are a special type of behavioural simulation. They are designed to help evaluate the candidate's skills in performing tasks directly related to the position. A typing or shorthand test for a secretary, driving test for a driver or a language test for a translator are examples of job replica tests.

## Targeted selection interviews

The objective of a targeted selection interview is to provide specific information about the candidate, on predefined dimensions that have been identified as important for a particular position. The employer identifies the critical skills, qualifications and personal traits needed to perform the job. The interview questions are designed in advance to target these areas and to allow for in-depth analysis of the candidate. The whole process is based on the assumption that past behaviour is the best indication of future behaviour.

A whole chapter in this book is devoted to these targeted areas: the most common questions are analysed in depth and possible answers suggested. Employers are not interested in theoretical or hypothetical answers. They want to hear your experience. Each example from your past has to address the following elements:

- The situation that existed (problem you had to solve or task you had to perform).
- The actions you took in order to solve the problem or perform the task.
- The result of your actions (the outcome of your efforts).

This evaluation method is becoming very popular with many companies, especially with the big players in the resources sector (mining, mineral processing, oil and gas). After a couple of interviews it became obvious to me that the same consultant had been used to devise a list of questions, for the lists were almost identical, and the emphasis placed on the same values. This makes it much easier for astute job hunters to prepare themselves for the interview.

To the applicant the major advantage of this interviewing technique is consistency. All applicants are asked the same questions, so they'll be judged by the same criteria. The main disadvantage is the lack of flexibility. Individual differences tend to be ignored or overlooked if the interviewers don't ask pertinent questions, probing for more revealing answers.

The applicants usually feel the rigid structure of this interview type tends to make them less relaxed, and the whole process is dominated by the interviewers.

A highly structured interview such as targeted selection is the most time-efficient of all types. For an inexperienced interviewer it is also the easiest one to conduct. That must be the reason for its survival in the battle against more efficient, flexible and intimate methods.

## Unstructured interviews

The unstructured or unguided interview is a less rigid encounter during which the applicant sets the pace and, to a certain extent, dictates the progress of the interview. Questions asked tend to follow the leads given by the applicant. This gives you the leading edge, puts the control in your hands and makes it much easier to expand on your strong points and avoid problem areas. This interview type tends to be used by two groups of recruiters – the inexperienced greenhorns and the very experienced head hunters.

The first group uses it for the simple reason that they can't control the interview so they leave it to the candidate to set the pace and sell themselves. Experienced interviewers, on the other hand, use this technique to evaluate, above other attributes, the candidate's character and personal traits. They can read between the lines and make conclusions not only about what the applicant said, but also about things that the applicant *did not* mention, either because of not knowing how to say it or because they were concealing something.

# Evaluation methods: the mystery revealed

It is far from easy to evaluate a person in an hour or so. Résumés, interview formats, evaluation methods, psychological tests, reference checks and a whole range of other tools have been used by employers in the selection process. In order to compare applicants, identify their strong and weak points and match them against the predefined criteria for a particular job, various evaluation methods have been developed by recruiting personnel.

## Basic concerns

There are three basic concerns for employers when recruiting.

1 Can the candidate do the job?
2 Will the candidate do the job?
3 Will the candidate fit into the workplace team?

Your task is to convince and reassure the employer that the answer to each of these questions is *yes*!

## Areas for evaluation

There is no universal evaluation method that could be applied to every applicant and to every position. Different employers place different values on the same skills and abilities. However, there are dimensions that are common to almost every evaluation method. Let us take a look at some of them and identify the employer's line of thinking when assessing your background.

1 **Qualifications:** Has the applicant the formal qualifications to do the job? Does he know how to do the job? Are his qualifications recognized in the industry as appropriate for this particular kind of position?

2 **Work experience:** Has the applicant relevant work experience? How much experience does she have and how could we benefit from that experience?

3 **Motivation:** How motivated is the candidate? What motivates him – money, sense of achievement, praise, title, working conditions? Is he a self-starter or does he need constant supervision?

4 **Communication skills:** Can the candidate express herself in writing and in good grammatical form? Can she express herself in individual and group situations orally? Is she a good listener? Can she effectively communicate her ideas and explain and present tasks?

5 **Maturity and emotional stability:** Is the candidate able to cope with stress and pressures at work and in private life? Is he a mature and responsible person who can make decisions and assume responsibility? Is he emotionally stable and fair and consistent in his dealings with superiors and subordinates?

6 **Sound health:** How good is the candidate's health? Is she likely to be productive for a long time? Is she going to be on sick leave more than usual and claim above average amounts on hospital benefits and from workers' compensation?

## The information employers need

The aim of job interviews – and especially targeted selection interviews – is to collect job-related behaviour examples from the applicants' history. The interviewers require three types of information for each example in order to evaluate the candidate:

1 The situation that existed or task that had to be performed.
2 The specific action taken or not taken (and why).
3 The results or consequences of the action (or the lack of it).

Interviewers using this method have to make sure that only complete examples are collected. You, the candidate, have to frame your answers accordingly and address all three issues.

## Incomplete answers

By using this method employers try to eliminate 'non-genuine' answers, which don't reflect candidate's past experience. 'False' answers could be classified as follows:

- Vague answers
- Theoretical answers
- Future-oriented answers
- Incomplete answers.

Vague answers lack clarity, simplicity, coherence or focus on the issue. Applicants quite often omit some relevant detail, either intentionally (if the information is unfavourable) or unintentionally.

Most applicants are good in giving theoretical answers. It isn't difficult to tell the interviewer what you would do in a certain situation, what you could do to solve a problem or how you would handle an obstacle. In most cases the answer is obvious to an experienced interviewee. This is where attentive listening to the way interviewers phrase questions and looking for clues in their behaviour is invaluable.

Future-oriented answers tell the employer what you are planning to do in future. This information is not necessarily useless, but since most employers tend to predict future behaviour on the basis of your past performance, the future-oriented answers are perceived as much less important than required 'factual' answers.

Incomplete answers lack one or more of the three main components (situation or task that the applicant performed, action taken by applicant or results of that action).

## Psychological and aptitude tests

What is the point of giving the applicants a psychological test that bears no relation to the job they have been considered for? How do we define 'personality'? Which personalities are suited to which jobs? What happens with multiple-choice questions when there is no suggested option that matches the true feeling of the candidate?

These and many other questions started the debates about the relevance of psychological and aptitude tests in the recruiting process and led to their ban in the USA. Basically, they did not meet the requirements of the equal-opportunity laws. The tests tried to asses the applicants' personalities and their suitability for particular jobs by asking vague questions that were open to interpretation and enabled employers to justify their opinions, biases and final choices. However, don't be surprised if some employers get you to spend a couple of hours behind closed doors, ticking off boxes and doing quick sums.

We don't have enough space here to explain all tests and methods in detail, so let's just take a quick look at the main types of tests, as expertly presented in the book *Effective Recruitment & Selection Practices*, by R.L. Crompton and A.R. Nankervis:

- General ability tests, which measure verbal, numerical, speed, spatial, strength, co-ordination or perceptual skills.
- Specific aptitude tests or work sample, such as keyboard, technical, foreign language, etc, skills.
- Personality (or temperament) tests, which are designed to assess overall 'personality' characteristics such as 'introversion versus extroversion', 'initiative' or 'creativity'.

It is essential to mention here the two basic types of testing: psychometric and psychodynamic. Psychometric tests compare the individual with a standard population profile defined by test standards. In psychodynamic testing, the emphasis is placed on the way a person reacts; therefore it represents a more qualitative approach than psychometric testing.

Some of the most popular tests used are The Defence Mechanism Test (DMT), which originates in Sweden, The Ravens test, The Watson–Glaser Test, and The Colour Test.

- In the DMT test, a candidate is given a large sheet of paper with 20 empty squares. In a split second a slide appears in a box. The candidate, looking into the box, has to draw their impression of the picture on the slide.
- The Ravens Test uses a set of matrices of increasing complexity, in order to test a candidate's visual problem-solving ability.
- The Watson–Glaser Test in a similar way tests a candidate's ability to think logically, solve problems, evaluate information and make decisions.
- In The Colour Test, candidates have to arrange differently coloured tiles in accordance to a few rules. The final product is two pyramids, whose pattern reveals details about candidates' characters and intellectual inclinations.

# 05 do's and don'ts in interviewing

**In this chapter you will learn:**
- what to do and what not to do in preparation for an interview
- what to do and what not to do during an interview
- what to do and what not to do after an interview

# Before the interview

- Study this book.
- Research the company you are, or will be, interviewing with.
- Find out as much as possible about the job you've applied for.
- Prepare your own customized answers based on the model answers in the next chapter and on the particulars of the job.
- Practise your answers, either alone or with a partner playing the role of the interviewer. If needed, record your sessions on a video or audio tape and try to improve your accent, diction, tone of voice and fluency.
- Prepare your interview clothes and try all combinations. Select the outfit that complies with normal business standards and allows you to feel comfortable and confident while wearing it.
- A day or two before the interview, visit the premises you'll be interviewed in, to assess the travelling time and to familiarize yourself with the surroundings. You'll feel more comfortable when you arrive for the interview.
- Arrange to have the interview at the best time for you. If you feel your best in the morning, don't arrange the interview for the afternoon. Avoid Mondays and Fridays if possible – the interviewers may feel rushed, tired or irritated.
- Check the condition of your car or the public transport timetable, to allow for unpredictable events. Being late for an interview is a mortal sin.
- Do anything necessary to improve your looks: have a haircut, trim your beard (men), manicure your nails, whiten your teeth.
- Have a light snack. Never walk into an interview on an empty stomach. Don't eat too much, either. The last thing you need is feeling sleepy or sluggish before and during the show.
- If you're a nervous person or just 'stage shy' have a cup of strong black coffee. Caffeine is a stimulant and can give you an extra edge. I personally used capsules with herbal extracts for their tranquillizing effect. Both methods are good, but you have to be careful not to take too much. Experiment beforehand.
- While waiting for the interview to start, practise relaxation techniques. Breathe deeply and try to relax.
- If your palms sweat, make sure they are dry when you shake hands with the interviewer. Sweaty palms are the first bad impression people usually make.

# During the interview

- Be businesslike and professional.
- Don't talk too much.
- Listen carefully and watch for clues. Feedback from the interviewer is a valuable tool in framing your answers.
- Use strong, positive reasons when explaining gaps and changes in your career.
- Be truthful, but be prepared to 'bend' the truth if it suits the circumstances. However, project honesty and sincerity.
- Ask relevant questions that will help you look intelligent, educated and experienced. Your questions should make the interviewer aware that you have done some research on the company, which will help you to be seen as an ambitious and resourceful person.
- Never take any books to an interview, especially not this one or any other on interviewing or job hunting.
- Establish and maintain eye contact with the interviewer.
- Smile. Be friendly and relaxed. Project optimism.
- Don't try to sell yourself too strongly.
- Never criticize your previous or present employers.
- Never indicate that you are desperate to get a job.
- Never make jokes.
- Never bring your friend, spouse, children or anybody else with you to the interview, not even to the waiting room.
- Never talk about your personal life, business secrets or the internal affairs of other companies, such as your present or former employers. Trustworthiness is a rare commodity and the interviewer will appreciate the fact that you may refuse (by politely avoiding the answer) to answer some questions.
- Sit straight in your chair or lean slightly forward. That way you project interest and attention.
- Never play with your keys, hair, tie, watch, pen or any other item.
- Don't fidget with your hands, drum your fingers, keep your hands in you pockets, scratch your head or crack your knuckles.
- Never eat, drink, smoke, chew gum or pick your teeth.
- Never wear dark glasses, a hat or dental braces.
- Make sure you don't smell of alcohol, garlic or any other strong odour.

- Don't make comments about the interviewer's office, furnishings, the receptionist, air-conditioner, etc.
- Never answer a question if you don't understand it fully. Ask for further clarification.
- Never use phrases such as 'I don't know', 'I don't think so', 'I disagree', 'What kind of question is that?', 'Why do you want to know that?' or any similar statement or question.
- Bring the conversation to a human level. Don't just plainly supply the information the interviewer wants to hear. Use examples, feelings, analogies, comparisons ... Use fresh words, not the usual common phrases and clichés.
- Be persuasive. Speak in terms of the benefits to the employer of hiring you. Talk in terms of their requirements.
- If you don't know an answer to a particular question, openly admit it. Don't be tempted to answer the question. Nobody knows everything.
- Never use the interviewer's first name. Adjust the formality of your behaviour to suit the interviewer's.
- If you feel that the interviewer is insulting you or if you feel manipulated, leave immediately. Your dignity should be more important than any job. If they treat you that way before offering you a job, can you imagine what your life would be like once you start working for them?
- Never bring up the question of salary and benefits yourself. Wait for the interviewer to start discussing money matters, otherwise you may be viewed as interested only in money. When negotiating your salary, make sure that you don't mention the amount first. Whoever comes up with a first figure is disadvantaged in the negotiation process.
- Although some specialists on interviewing disagree, I think it is good practice to take notes during the interview (of course, only while the interviewer is speaking). This should help you in case you have to come back for a second interview or to evaluate the job later, should you have more then one job offer. Just make sure you don't overdo it. Your notes should be as brief as possible to enable you to maintain an eye contact with the interviewer at all times.

# After the interview

- Always write a polite 'Thank you' note to the interviewer. Consider the format shown opposite.
- Record all details about the interview in your 'job file' as soon as possible, preferably immediately after the interview. That can prove extremely valuable in the future, for it will enable you to evaluate your performance and avoid costly mistakes. The following information should prove useful:
  - the name of the company and the interviewer;
  - general impression of the company, the job and the interviewer;
  - specific interviewer's questions and areas of interest;
  - interviewer's feedback and reactions to your answers;
  - interviewer's comments about your résumé, your education or employment history;
  - specific job-related information supplied by the interviewer;
  - the interviewer's body language and non-verbal communication.
- Immediately after the interview, analyse your performance and write down your specific comments and self-impressions. They will be extremely valuable in preparation for job interviews in future. You may even have another interview with the same company in the near future. These are some of the points you should cover in your post-interview self-appraisal:
  - your best answers (judging by your interpretation of the interviewer's response);
  - your poorest answers;
  - your body language and behaviour;
  - your questions, their relevance and appropriateness;
  - other relevant details (whether you arrived on time, the way you greeted the interviewer, etc.);
  - the things you would change or introduce if you could do it again.
- Be persistent. If you were unsuccessful interviewing with a particular employer, don't automatically assume that the company has no openings for you. Just a couple of months later, you might be called in for another interview.

Arthur Renton
25 Bridge Street
Canandigua, NY 14424


Mrs Ann Kennedy
Roberts and Partners
1034 Avenue of the Americas
New York, New York 10020


26 August, 2000



Dear Mrs Kennedy,

Thank you for the opportunity to talk to you about the position
of Litigation Lawyer with your firm. After discussing this career
opportunity with you I feel that Roberts and Partners is the right
environment for me to utilize my skills and knowledge and
contribute to your company's success.

I would be proud to be associated with such a reputable firm and
consider it a privilege to be on your team.

Yours sincerely,



Arthur Renton

I had three interviews with my present employer in two years. Although I was unsuccessful on the first two occasions for various reasons, the third interview resulted in a job offer. The experience I gained in the first two interviews (although with different interviewers) enabled me to think in terms of benefits to the employer, to prepare my answers and polish up my performance for the third and final encounter. I was selected for the job amongst more than 40 applicants, some probably better experienced and qualified for the job than I was. By the time I had the last interview, I had prepared a folder containing crucial information – the questions I was asked, the answers I gave, the names of interviewers, as well as many important details about the company, its operations and philosophy. Before the third appraisal, I studied the available information and prepared myself properly. My preparations obviously paid off.

# 06

## questions, answers and eye-openers

**In this chapter you will learn:**
- some typical interview questions with sample responses
- advice on how to approach some of the trickier 'knockout' questions

*Hard questions must have hard answers.*

Plutarch

This chapter deals with some typical interview questions. There is only a limited number of questions you could be asked to answer. They may vary slightly in content, interviewer's tone of voice or accent, order of questions, but the best answers will always be the best answers.

Behind each question you have to recognize the interviewer's fear or concern, which is basically the reason they are asking you the question. Once you have established that reason you can frame the optimal answers accordingly. My comments, printed in italics, may help you do that.

For most questions I have suggested a skeleton you might like to consider using in your answers. You can expand on it or change it to suit your background. Don't change it drastically: use it as a starting point for your script. For some questions only short advice is given, because those questions require specific answers which will reflect your occupation or experience.

The interviewer's task is to evaluate various areas of your background, such as your work experience, education, communication skills, salary history, management skills, etc. The questions in this chapter are grouped together according to those areas. The order of questions asked will vary from interview to interview.

There are at least half a dozen questions in each area. There will be no need for an interviewer to ask you all of them, so you can use certain answers in answering other, related questions. Sometimes the question you'll be asked will comprise two questions in one, or even three or more (less likely, but possible). In this case make sure you remember all the questions you were asked and answer them one by one. Most people just answer the first one and forget about the rest. Some interviewers use this tactic (asking a few questions together) to test the candidate's memory and concentration.

Some questions are more important than others because of the impact they may have on the interviewer. I call them 'knockout' questions because of their potential to get you out of the job game very quickly if not answered properly. Pay special attention to these questions. Most interviewers use them for initial evaluation; should you 'pass' this hard part, you'll be a serious candidate for the job. Should you 'fail', you could see an abrupt end to the interview.

*As with any performance, such as acting or public speaking (job interview has elements of both), practice is of paramount importance. It's not enough to know the answers. You must be able to deliver them in the best possible way.*

The system is simple – record the questions and your own answers on tape. Play it in your spare time. Once you've remembered all questions and all answers, make another tape. This time record only the questions, leaving time for you to answer them. Do that in front of a mirror, observing your body language and 'delivery'.

*Perfect practice makes perfect performance.*

## Personal details

1   **Do you have a valid driver's licence?**
    *If you have a valid licence:*
A:  Yes, I have a full licence, which is valid until (*give date*).
    *If you don't already have a driver's licence, say you'll get one.*

2   **Have you ever been convicted for a driving offence?**
    *If you have, explain the circumstances and determination not to allow it to happen again.*
A:  I always drive carefully and never drink alcohol before driving. Once I was in a hurry to be on time for an appointment and lost one point for driving just above the speed limit. Otherwise my driving record is clean.

3   **Do you have any chronic health conditions or disabilities?**
    *This question is illegal, and you do not have to answer it. If you choose to answer, consider something along these lines:*
A:  My health is generally very good. I exercise regularly and control my weight. I have had (*slightly high blood pressure, diabetes, asthma …*) for a few years but I control it, so I haven't had any of the usual symptoms and it has never affected my performance at work.
    *or*
    My health is excellent. I have no chronic health conditions (*a much better answer*).

4    Do you own a car? If so, what make and model?

A:   At the moment I don't have a car, because I have sold my old one, but if the job requires the use of a reliable and presentable car I am prepared to buy one as soon as possible.

*or*

I own a _____ (*make and model of car*) free of debt.

5    Have you done any military service?

*Emphasize your achievements during any military service you have undertaken, especially the ones that, in some way, relate to the job you are being interviewed for.*

6    How far do you live from this office?

A:   I live only eleven kilometres from the office. It took me just over 18 minutes to get here, which is very good if you take into account that it was the rush hour.

7    This job would require you to move to another part of the country. Would that be a problem?

*Point out that you knew about the job requirements and that you are prepared to move anywhere (if you are).*

A:   I was aware of that fact before I applied for this position, so I discussed the issue with my partner, who would like to move to _____ (*place*) as much as I would. The atmosphere of the city is very similar to our present lifestyle and we have some very good friends there, so it shouldn't take us long to get acclimatized.

8    I can see from your résumé that you speak German and Italian. How proficient are you in those languages?

A:   I studied German in primary school and in high school and found the language interesting, so I studied it further through language courses and tapes. I even spent a summer working in Germany and improving my proficiency, so now I'm fluent in German.

*or*

My partner is a foreign language teacher and has taught me basic Italian. I'm not very fluent, but I can read and write the language quite well.

9    Are you a member of a trades union?

*If a job requires a membership in a particular union, say you will apply for it immediately (if you are not a member already). If the employer's general attitude is to oppose the unions, emphasize the fact that you are purely a financial member, with no involvement in union activities.*

**A:** I have been a member of the union for the past six years but I'm not active in the union movement or activities.

# Education and training

*Colleges can't produce competence, but they can produce graduates.*

Anon.

**1  What college/university did you attend?**

**A:** I attended _____ school (*your school*) in _____. After graduation I enrolled at _____ (*the university you attended*). I graduated with honours from the Faculty of _____.

**2  Why did you choose that particular institution?**

*Most employers value practical skills much more than the theoretical ones. Emphasize that aspect in your answer.*

**A:** I selected that university because of its competitive atmosphere and the outstanding reputation of the _____ (*Engineering Department, Arts School ...*). The courses were well balanced, with just the right mixture of theoretical and practical topics. It encouraged student participation in different activities and emphasized practical skills that can be applied to problems in industry.

**3  Did your family have any influence on your choice of career?**

*Stress the fact that **you** chose your occupation. Having parents making decisions for you is a serious knockout factor.*

**A:** My parents made some suggestions, but they never tried to influence my decisions. They realized that I had made up my mind and that I knew what I wanted so they left me to decide.

**4  What was your major?**

**A:** I majored in _____ (*interior design, maintenance management, English literature ...*). I have always liked the challenges and satisfaction of that demanding but interesting discipline.

**5  Do you think you made the right career choice?**

*For people staying in the same occupation:*

**A:** I am very pleased with my decision. Although I have other talents I am sure this profession suits my abilities well and enables me to fully utilize my knowledge and skills. It gives me a great sense of achievement and the rewards are adequate.

*For people who are changing careers or are contemplating a change:*

When I started my career as _____ (*a lawyer, interior designer ...*) I kept learning and growing on the job. After mastering the skills and achieving my goals in that area, I decided to gain additional experience in _____ (*mention the occupation you want to move into*). That way my creativity and flexibility was enhanced and I have achieved a range of new skills that I can use in my new career.

6  **Do you feel your education prepared you well for the challenges in the work force?**

A: My education and training gave me a solid foundation on which I built my knowledge base and gave me the confidence to face the future challenges. To achieve good results at university I had to work hard, set my goals and do my best to achieve them. The same principles apply in the work force. The problem-solving and goal-setting skills that I acquired have helped me throughout my career.

7  **How did you do in school?**

A: My grades were above average, always in the top fifteen per cent of my class. I worked part-time as well and was involved in many extracurricular activities, in student clubs and societies.

8  **How did you finance your education?**

*If you worked part-time to pay the fees, tell them so. It shows your determination and willingness to work hard. Scholarships, grants and stipends are not bad either. Your talents must have been recognized earlier, otherwise you wouldn't have got it.*

A: Throughout my college days I worked part-time to pay expenses. My parents helped a great deal and I also received a scholarship from _____.

9  **What were your favourite subjects/courses?**

*Mention something related to the position you are being interviewed for.*

A: I always felt great interest towards (*commerce, marketing ...*), but when I took that course I discovered challenges and possibilities in that area. Other related courses reinforced my interest for the subject and I found I had the potential to be successful in that field.

10 **Did you ever need tutoring? In what subjects?**
*Even if you did use a tutor, don't mention it. That information cannot be checked and is not relevant to your current abilities and skills.*

A: I didn't need tutoring or any other help. I attended lectures and tutorials regularly and never had any particular difficulties.

11 **How much knowledge gained in school do you feel you could use on this job?**
*Ideally, all of it. Practically, only some of it. Your answer should be closer to 'all of it'.*

A: This position requires knowledge and some of the skills I acquired as a student. Most of the courses I studied could be directly related to this job. My knowledge of _____ and especially my background in _____ would enable me to carry out all tasks required on this job very successfully.

12 **What courses in school gave you the most difficulty?**
*Mention some subject or area that is totally irrelevant to the job you are applying for.*

A: I never felt a great deal of interest for _____ (*history, foreign languages, classic literature ...*), but I forced myself to study hard so I managed to achieve above average results.

13 **What courses were the easiest ones for you?**
*Again, use the courses that can be directly related to the job.*

A: I've always liked _____ (*mathematics, physics, typing, computer programming ...*). I felt a great deal of pleasure preparing for those exams and my results were outstanding. Those courses were a solid foundation for my later studies and equipped me with practical skills that I used later on the job.

14 **Are you planning to continue your studies towards _____ (a diploma/degree/higher degree/MBA/PhD)?**

A: After beginning my career I realized that in addition to my degree in _____ (*engineering, geology, law ...*), I needed some general business and management skills, so in (*1996, 1997 ...*) I enrolled at the MBA programme at _____. I expect to graduate in two years time. I'm putting my new skills to use applying them to my job in order to handle demanding tasks more efficiently.

15 **Have you received any formal training since graduation?**

*By asking this question the interviewer wants to see whether you have continued to expand and update your knowledge and skills. This is a good opportunity to score points.*

**A:** After graduation I used every opportunity to expand my knowledge and acquire further skills. I attended various courses, workshops and seminars. Most of them were accredited courses, recognized by _____ (*The Institution of Engineers, The Association of Chartered Accountants.* ...). Some of them were sponsored by my employers and for others I used my own time and money. The investment in training has really paid off, because it has enabled me to become more efficient and master new skills that I could directly apply on the job.

*or*

So far I have used every opportunity to improve my knowledge and skills through on-the-job learning and subscribing to trade magazines. This year I'm planning to enrol in a _____ course to enhance my knowledge on the subject.

# Personal traits

*If any young man comes to me and asks how to make his fortune, I tell him to do the same. Don't follow everybody else. Get off the beaten track. Be a little mad.*

Jeno Paulucci, *How It Was to make $100 Million in a Hurry*

## Attention to detail

1 **Do you occasionally get bored while doing detailed work?**

*If you're applying for a manual job or a job that involves detailed work (design, finance, craftsmanship ...) this is a very appropriate question. Even if you apply for a supervisory job or a position in management (more oriented towards problem solving and decision making), you will occasionally have to deal with details.*

**A:** I treat all my activities as an extension of the job. My daily routine requires efficiency to increase the results achieved. This efficiency includes devoting attention to details. If people couldn't get the little things right, how could they expect to do the big things? So, no matter how busy I am, working on concepts and bigger issues, I always make checking details high priority.

**2  Do you like analytical tasks?**

**A:**  I consider myself very good at facts and figures. I developed my mathematical and analytical skills early and have been using them for quite some time. My decision to become _____ (*an accountant, a statistician, an engineer* ...) reflected that orientation towards facts and figures. I like the organized way of thinking and the systematic approach to problems needed when dealing with facts and figures. These skills help me in all spheres of my job.

**3  What methods do you use for controlling errors in your paperwork?**

**A:**  Since the introduction of personal computers and software packages such as spreadsheets and word processors, it has become much easier to control errors and mistakes. As I progress through a project, I make sure I regularly check all facts and figures and update the necessary paperwork. If some typing is done by my secretary, I proofread it and make sure there are no errors before signing it.

**4  Tell me about a time when you or your superiors found an error in your work. What was the outcome of the whole situation?**

**A:**  I haven't made many errors in my work, due to my attention to detail and the attention I pay to all aspects of a certain task. Occasionally, when jobs had to be finished in a very short time or when not enough information was available, some minor error would creep in. On one occasion I prepared figures for a next-day presentation. Just before the meeting a calculation error was discovered, so I had to correct it urgently. Fortunately, it occurred later in the process, so only a minor part of the material had to be changed and everything ended well.

**5  Do you get bored or lose interest in doing the same tasks over and over again?**

**A:**  Daily routine is more or less part of everybody's job. If my job involves repetitive work it is my responsibility to carry it out to the best of my abilities. There are some tasks that have to be done regularly and I don't regard them as boring or unchallenging. I consider every task as important and due to my workload I'm never bored or idle.

## Energy

1  **When do you tend to do your best work, in the morning or in the afternoon?**

*Most of us have a favourite period, when we feel best and tend to produce our best results. This question, however, tries to assess your energy level. Make sure you don't say things like: 'I do most work in the morning, because I feel exhausted after lunch and need some rest'.*

A:  The time of day usually has no impact on my efficiency and energy level, but I prefer morning hours for major tasks, and late afternoon or early evening for planning, design and catching up on paperwork. I rarely get tired, even when I work overtime – it's just that some periods during the day are better suited for particular activities.

2  **How do you catch up on a work backlog after a holiday or absence from site?**

*Apart from testing your energy level, this question probes into your organizational skills. Frame your answer in a way that highlights your systematic approach in prioritizing issues and tasks.*

A:  In a situation like this, I try to spend a few hours in the office the day before I officially start work, be it Sunday or during the working week. That way I can go through the mail and messages, sort them in order of importance and urgency and plan my activities for the week ahead. The first few days after my return are always very busy. There are people to talk to, many messages to be answered and issues to be resolved. That usually requires a lot of overtime, but that has always been a part of my work day, especially after long absence.

3  **What do you do with your spare time? What do you do for exercise?**

A:  I always try to spend my free time with my family. We play sports, go for walks, do some gardening or work around the house. In the evenings I pursue my hobbies or catch up on my reading. I exercise in the morning, by doing long walks combined with jogging and some weightlifting.

4  **What kind of tasks do you find most tiring?**

*Because of the way this question is formed, it's a bit tricky to answer it favourably. Your message has to be based on the fact that you don't tire easily, no matter what kind of task you are dealing with.*

5   **Have you worked on night shifts before?**

A:   I have worked night shifts often in the past. If this job requires night shift work that would suit me fine.

*or*

So far I haven't worked on a night shift. However, I often worked long hours and afternoon shifts, so if this job requires some night shift work I could do it without any problems.

6   **What are the longest hours you have ever worked?**
*The answer will depend on your occupation and your particular circumstances. Don't just say: 'twelve hours'. Explain the problem, the urgency of the situation, the skills you used at the time, etc. Expand and explain.*

A:   On quite a few occasions, when an urgent or important problem had to be solved or a critical task done, such as _____ (*major plant shutdown, urgent surgery, major equipment failure ...*) I worked very long hours, typically _____ (*twelve, sixteen, twenty ...*) hours. In my profession it is necessary to put in long hours quite often so the job can be done on time.

## Initiative and creativity

*There is nothing more difficult to carry out, nor more doubtful of success, nor more dangerous to handle, then to initiate a new order of things.*

Niccolo Machiavelli

---

- Taking active steps to achieve goals.
- Active attempts to initiate action, rather then passively observing.
- Doing things differently and more efficiently.
- Attempts to achieve more than originally called for.

Key words: ambition, drive, motivation, self-starter, innovation, peak performance.

1 **Have you ever worked alone or without direct supervision?**
*The ability to work alone is perceived as very important by interviewers. Nobody wants to employ candidates who need a supervisor to keep telling them what to do, when, how and why.*

A: In my former job as construction foreman, I have worked long hours in remote areas without direct supervision. Occasionally, I would consult a site engineer regarding some technical problem, but generally I handled all problems and managed the work group by myself.

2 **What have you done in your current job to make it more productive or challenging?**
*This is the right time to mention ideas that you've implemented and new projects or innovations you have made at your place of work. Be specific and address the three basic elements: situation (problem), your action and the outcome.*

3 **Do you think you are an innovative person? Why do you think so?**

A: I certainly try to be innovative. Whenever I have a task to accomplish or have to solve a problem, I think about different ways that can lead towards the successful completion of that task or solution to the problem. Most of the time people choose the easiest solution, they use a path of least resistance, but in the majority of cases the easiest solutions are not the best. I enjoy investigating new possibilities, considering new ways of doing things and using new methods to achieve objectives.

4 **Give me some examples of projects or tasks when you did more than normally required in your job.**
*By asking this question the interviewer will try to establish how you define a good job and evaluate your work standards.*

A: To achieve peak performance, I always put in more effort than merely doing the job by the book. This comes naturally to me, as part of my work ethics. I am not happy with mediocre efforts, because they lead to mediocre results.
*Add an example or two from your own experience to support this opening.*

5   Tell me about some projects you generated or initiated yourself.

*The ability to recognize problems and issues that need attention and to take action in solving or rectifying them is regarded as important by many employers. You have to convince them in your answer that you are not just a passive observer and follower, but rather a resourceful person and a self-starter.*

6   Have you found any ways of making your staff's jobs easier or more interesting?

*This question is intended for people who control and manage a group of people. There are many new management ideas and methods, with the purpose of making jobs more interesting and challenging. You can mention a successful implementation of some of those schemes or programmes, such as an employee participation scheme which involved the whole group in the decision-making process, something like a competition challenge between shifts or teams, or schemes such as 'The Employee of the Month Award'. Anything original and innovative will be a big plus for you.*

7   Are there some methods that you use that are different or some things that you do differently than other (accountants, managers, sales staff ...)?

*Being original and innovative is always nice, just make sure you don't overdo it. You may be seen as unpredictable, a misfit or a weirdo. Concentrate on relatively uncommon, not very 'exotic' methods or work practices.*

A:  Each creative person has his or her own techniques and means for achieving results and getting the job done, as well as little secrets that sometimes mean big success. None of them is universal and suitable for everybody. What works for you may not work for me, and vice versa.

*Now talk about one or two of your 'specialties'; things or methods that you use because they work well for you.*

## Integrity

*You've got to stand for something, or you're going to fall for anything.*

John Cougar Mellencamp

---

- Maintaining and observing social, ethical and organizational norms in job-related activities.
- The quality of being honest and upright in character.

---

1 **To get the job done people sometimes have to bend the truth. Give me an example when you had to do that.**

*A typical knockout question. By asking the question this way, the interviewer indicates that such behaviour is common and not necessarily negative – and even condones it. Don't fall into this trap. By doing this they want you to admit an instance of low integrity behaviour. Fair play and personal integrity are still highly valued by interviewers, especially the ones of British origin. The American credo is to win; the British motto is to participate.*

2 **Have you ever broken some company rule?**

*Another knockout question. Some employers are very sensitive when their rules, policies and procedures are concerned. They become so indoctrinated that any individualistic approach or alternative way of doing things is viewed as a major disloyalty and disobedience. Your answer here has to be: never!*

A: I consider company rules, policies and procedures necessary for efficient running of the business. They ensure that fairness, consistency and safety measures are applied across the board and that the right work environment is created and maintained. My personal policy is to always observe the rules and make sure my subordinates observe them as well.

3 **Some sales people frequently tend to 'oversell' the product to make a sale. What is your opinion of that technique?**

A: I have never used the 'overselling' technique. My philosophy in selling is that customers deserve unbiased and honest advice on products and services. Anyone who misleads the buyers creates a very negative image for the company and himself and loses credibility, which is one of the most precious attributes in business.

4 **Have you ever done any foolish things?**
*In your answer, stick to your childhood days. Give them an example from that period. Unless you are being interviewed for a position in a circus, tell them you haven't done any foolish things. You always think before you act and always assume full responsibility for your actions.*

A: Although I don't mind a laugh every now and then, I think there is no room for foolishness in the workplace. My attitude has always been one of maturity, reliability and professionalism. I always consider all pros and cons before taking action and avoid acting impulsively or immaturely.

## Job motivation

1 **Can you name a few things that motivate you in your job?**

A: I have always been self-motivated. I like the winning feeling when I do a good job and the sense of achievement and job satisfaction motivates me to make even bigger efforts. I also like being around people who are capable, hard working and good team players. I enjoy interaction with my co-workers and the team spirit.

2 **Tell me about an instance when you worked hard and felt proud of your achievement.**
*This question is similar to question 4 below. You can use the same frame, with additional emphasis on factors that were additional sources of motivation in those instances.*

3 **What were your reasons for leaving your last job?**

A: My last job was an interesting and creative one. It provided daily challenges and required hard work. Initially, I was learning a lot, but then I realized that I was specializing in a very narrow field and lacking skills and experience in other aspects of _____ (*sales, human, resources, law ...*). I also realized that I would have to broaden my skills and experience to be able to handle the demands future developments might bring.

4 **What were the most important events or persons in your career development?**

A: My career development started during my school days. My _____ (*mathematics, art, English ...*) teacher recognized my talents for _____ (*figures, drawing, literature ...*) and had a big influence on my choice of career by encouraging me to excel in that area. At university, my tutor helped me learn a lot about the subject and taught me many valuable lessons. At work I had the privilege to work with and learn from a few brilliant _____ (*surgeons, solicitors, graphic artists* ...). The experience I gained during that period prepared me well for the challenges that lie ahead.

5   **Who was the best boss you ever worked for?**

*The interviewer wants to know what type of person gets the most out of you and what type of people you like working with. Talking about people we like is very revealing. It tells them more about you than about those people! Another important aspect is the opportunity to learn from your former boss. Someone who has never worked for a good boss has missed a lot by not having a model on how to be a good boss.*

A:   The best boss I worked with was fair and consistent. She expected a lot from me, but also gave a lot in return. She taught me many necessary skills and work methods and provided a constant motivation and encouragement for my efforts. She didn't dictate what had to be done and when, but rather left it for me to decide and even make some minor mistakes in the process. It was all part of my training. We always felt mutual respect and trusted each other, and remain good friends. I consider myself very fortunate for having this person by my side early in my career, as a supervisor, teacher and remarkable person. She served as a role model for me and helped me develop my own leadership and interpersonal skills.

6   **Describe the worst boss you ever worked for.**

*Slippery ground. Remember the rule 'Never badmouth your former employers'? Explain systematically what that person's problems were and make sure you emphasize that everybody felt the same, that it wasn't just you who had problems dealing with him or her. Mention the steps you took to improve the relationship between the two of you and the successful outcomes of your efforts (if any).*

7   **Why did you choose this particular career?**

A:   My interest in _____ (*your field of work*) goes back to my school days. I displayed strong _____ (*list important skills needed on the job and in your profession*) skills and the decision to enter this profession came as a natural progression from that early interest. I regard this field as a challenging and an interesting one, with many demands and lot of hard work, but also full of opportunities and rewards for a job well done. It suits my capabilities and career plans, and I would think twice before changing my career path.

8   **What areas of your job and career do you like most?**
*Frame your answer to suit the position you are being interviewed for. If it's a job as a project engineer, emphasize your inclination towards design work, budget control, dealing with customers and consultants, etc. If the job involves sales, highlight your interest in contact with customers, travel, and so on.*

9   **How would you describe the ideal company? The company you would most like to work for?**
*It is relatively easy to define an ideal place of work, but make sure you include some characteristics of the company you are being interviewed by in your answer. Some call it adulation, but I call it opportunity to score some important points. Consider the following introduction and finish that with some positive aspects of the interviewer's company.*

A:  The progressive company provides a challenging, stimulating and supporting atmosphere for its employees and their achievements. It's a safe place to work in and treats its employees fairly. People enjoy working there and give their best to achieve the company's goals and targets.

10  **How many hours a day do you work in your present job?**
*Even if you work only eight hours a day, mention the occasional overtime, the work you take home with you, assignments away from home, and so on. Employers like people with a habit of doing more than they are paid for. It makes them feel good.*

A:  My normal working hours are from _____ (*eight to five, nine to six ...*), but I sometimes work nine or ten hours a day or a few hours on a Saturday, due to my workload.

## Resilience

- The quality or ability of quickly recovering the original state of mind or condition after being stressed, pushed to the limit, disappointed, mistreated, neglected, criticized or rejected, while maintaining effectiveness.

1 **Tell me about some of the biggest disappointments in your career and how you coped with them.**

A: I couldn't say that I have had any big disappointments in my career. I've been doing the type of work I like and that makes a good use of my knowledge and experience. The only disappointing factor I've encountered so far are some people who don't share my enthusiasm and pride in hard work, and who don't have the drive needed to achieve targets and contribute to their employer's success. Those people are more interested in their salaries and pay rises and it is hard to get any co-operation from them. I am not saying that everybody should share my values and views, but an unprofessional and laid-back attitude has an impact on the work group and the whole department and its performance.

2 **Have you gained any benefits from your disappointments?**
*The message should be: You have learned a lot from your disappointments and mistakes. You never repeat a mistake. You always analyse what went wrong, when, how and why.*

A: I have learned a lot from mistakes, either my own or those of others. I wouldn't call them disappointments, just temporary set-backs. Whenever I made a mistake my first task was to analyse what went wrong and how it could had been prevented. That way I don't repeat mistakes and anticipate potential problems.

3 **What career or business would you consider if you were starting all over again?**
*There are two possible answers. If you are being interviewed for a job in the same industry, you would choose the same career again. For people changing careers, the answer will depend on the job they are applying for. If you want to go into marketing, the answer should be: marketing.*

A: If I had to choose my career again, I would make the same choice. I feel happy in my occupation and I think this profession suits me well. This is what I do best, it's the area in which I can achieve my goals and make a significant contribution to my employer.

4 **Have you ever been refused a promotion or a pay rise?**

A: I have never had to ask for promotion or a pay rise. My employers recognized the value of my contribution and increased my salary according to performance evaluations, which have always been favourable.

5  **Are you sensitive to criticism?**

**A:** If the criticism is warranted, I try to analyse the problem, whatever it is, and rectify it. If I feel that the criticism is unfair or without grounds, I try to establish the reason for such behaviour. If I feel that I'm doing something right, I don't pay too much attention to unwarranted criticism.

6  **We all feel frustrated or angry at times. Have you ever resigned in frustration?**

*Another knockout question. Tell them you walked out on a job and you will find yourself walking out from the interview without a job.*

**A:** No, I haven't. People who resign or give up when facing a problem or difficulty of any kind at work lack persistence and resilience. Whenever I had personal or work-related difficulties I resolved them successfully.

7  **If there was something about yourself that you would like to improve, what would it be?**

*This is a knockout question, too, although a well disguised one. Make sure you select some minor flaw or deficiency, the one that couldn't have a big impact on your chances to get a job. Paperwork is always a useful example, as are filing and record-keeping skills. You concentrate on how to achieve major targets and goals and in the process neglect the paperwork, but you finish it later. Some relatively harmless shortcoming like that would be a good example.*

## Stress management

1  **Under what working conditions do you produce your best results?**

**A:** Like any self-starter and achiever, I tend to produce the best results in the right work environment. By the right work environment I mean a harmonious one, where team members work together towards a common goal and concentrate their efforts to get the job done in the shortest possible time. Their intellectual and practical capabilities are challenged and put to test, and some pressure is present. That gives them a sense of urgency of the job and stretches their faculties to the limit. They have all the equipment necessary to do the job, and undivided support from their supervisor or manager. That is the environment in which people grow on the job and achieve tangible results.

2   **How well do you work under pressure?**

*This is a leading question. The answer is obvious. You thrive under pressure. Everybody knows that nobody likes working under pressure, yet they still keep asking this question.*

A:  Working under pressure can be very productive. It can release untapped resources, such as inner strength and energy and motivate people to excel themselves. I have worked under pressure quite often, due to the nature of my vocation. This includes tasks that had to be done urgently, with limited resources, on short notice; in most cases I had to make decisions quickly and act on those decisions. I work quite well under pressure and I regard it as an additional motivator on the job.

3   **Have you ever lost your temper at work?**

*The same story again. You never lose your temper. You are patient, understanding, easy to deal with and everybody likes you a lot.*

A:  By maintaining an open and positive approach to problems and potential conflicts I have managed to resolve occasional misunderstandings and disputes to the satisfaction of both parties. I work very well with my colleagues and never lose my temper. I regard that sort of behaviour as counterproductive and inappropriate. By losing your temper you cannot possibly resolve a problem – you can only make it worse.

4   **What kinds of pressure do you feel in your job?**

*The ability to work on urgent and demanding jobs, within budgetary constraints, on short notice, with limited resources, without sufficient information and with various types of people is highly regarded by employers. These are the pressures they are interested in.*

A:  There are various kinds of pressure in my job. The common one is when urgent and important jobs have to be done in minimum time, so production wouldn't suffer, or when goals and targets have to be achieved in a short time, within a limited budget or with a shortage of people. In most cases this kind of pressure provides motivation and tends to bring out the best in me.

5   **How do you relax after a hard day at work?**

*Your relaxation method should be perceived as active or semi-active. Don't just tell them that you hit the bed or sink into a recliner chair while watching a soap opera. Mention activities that project a constructive image and reflect high energy levels, such as walking, jogging, swimming, gardening, playing with the kids, etc.*

**6 Would you classify yourself as a hard-driving or relatively laid-back personality?**
*Naturally, you have to tell them that you're a hard-working, no-nonsense achiever. In today's competitive climate, being laid-back is not viewed favourably.*

**A:** When it comes to my job, I don't have time to be laid back. When I'm at work, I always give my best and try to achieve as much as possible. Of course, it is necessary to slow down from time to time, to analyse my performance and plan future activities. Then, the hard driving starts again. I have always been self-motivated, and not to work hard would be against my beliefs.

## Tenacity

- Staying with a position or sticking to the plan of action until the desired objective or final goal is achieved or no longer achievable within a reasonable time.

Key words: persistence, commitment, perseverance, overcoming obstacles and problems.

**1 What were the biggest problems that you faced at university/college?**
**A:** I didn't have any major problems at university. I enjoyed every minute of it, especially the constant interactions with people and the busy schedule. Some courses were difficult, but I worked hard and eventually succeeded.

**2 Tell me about some obstacles you have had to overcome in the past.**
**A:** To achieve success in life and reach my goals I have had to put in a lot of time and effort to overcome obstacles such as _____ (*studying part-time, learning a new language and adapting to a different culture, handling difficult people, the death of a parent/spouse/child*).

3   **Have you had an experience where you achieved your goal because you persisted for a length of time?**

A:  To get my university degree I had to study hard for _____ years (*give study period*) and pass more than _____ (*number*) exams. It required persistence, stamina and lots of hard work. All those efforts paid off, because I am able to use my knowledge and experience at work. The main reasons for my success are that I had my goal clearly in mind and had no doubts in the positive outcome. I believed in myself.

4   **Sometimes we do our best, but fail to reach the target. Tell me about your experiences related to that situation.**

*When answering this question make sure you emphasize that the cause for the failure wasn't you, but something else: unrealistic target, inadequate equipment or resources, short time …*

A:  I haven't had many failures of that kind in my career. The closest I got to it was during my involvement in a project when the project team faced a couple of problems such as _____ (*delays in equipment delivery, strikes/industrial actions, inadequate human resources, lack of funds …*). Although I managed to carry out my task to the best of my abilities and achieve most of the targets, the project was postponed.

## Work standards

- Positive traits: High personal standards, not satisfied with poor or average performance, high standards set for peers, subordinates and the whole organization, meeting deadlines and demands of the job.

1   **How do you define doing a good job in your profession?**

*This example is applicable to engineers, planners and supervisors in project management and control, but the format would be similar for other professions.*

A:  The basic standard performance indicator in project management is completion of projects on time and within budget, while complying with the applicable standards and regulations and in accordance with the project documentation (specifications, tenders, scope of work).

To me, a good job means one I'm proud of, that gives me a sense of achievement and internal satisfaction, and is in line with my professional reputation. A job well done is the one that sets new personal and organizational standards, serves as a reference or milestone for future similar undertakings and gives satisfaction and impeccable service to the end user, who is always the final judge of the product.

2　**There probably were some times when you were not satisfied with your performance. What have you done about it?**

*Whenever you tell them something that isn't totally positive about yourself, you have to follow up immediately to explain what steps you took to rectify the problem or improve your performance. This question is a typical example. The interviewer wants to hear that you can recognize a potential problem or a shortcoming and take action to correct it.*

3　**How often have you missed deadlines and what were the usual causes?**

A:　I very rarely miss deadlines, due to my planning and organizational skills and project-management abilities. My experience plays an important role in anticipating the problems and prevention of the things that could go wrong. Good planning and effective control over the work force and equipment is the most effective weapon in the battle with time and mounting costs. Unexpected events, however, do happen, and that is the time to revise a plan and take urgent measures. On a few occasions the project I was managing was late, mostly due to industrial action or unforeseen difficulties in sourcing and delivery of parts and equipment.

4　**Tell me about times when you were very pleased with the job you did. Why did you feel that way?**

A:　On quite a few occasions I have managed to achieve required _____ (*production targets, sales figures ...*) much more quickly than planned and with a significant surplus in the budget. I was pleased with my delegation and work allocation methods, for they contributed significantly to the successful completion of tasks.

5　**Give me an example of times when your supervisor talked to you about your performance.**

*The question doesn't specify poor performance, so use the opportunity to emphasize your favourable performance appraisals.*

6   How do you judge the performance of your staff? What are the differences between a good employee and an average one?

*This theoretical question calls for a classic answer. Read the section about 'ideal employees' and use the employer's views as your own. Even the worst employees know what 'good employee' means.*

A:  To judge the performance of others, one has first to establish the criteria that will be used in the process. Once those criteria are communicated to employees, they will know what aspects of their performance will be monitored. Some of my criteria include attendance record (punctuality, hours worked, number of days off sick), successful completion of projects and tasks (on time and within budget), loyalty to the company, the ability to work well with others and continuous improvement of skills and performance. Good employees assume responsibility and take action when the job has to be done. They always work to the best of their abilities and can be trusted and relied upon in difficult times.

7   Have you ever dismissed an employee for not performing adequately? What were the circumstances?

A:  I have recently fired an employee because of her poor performance. She couldn't adopt the company work standards, despite working to the best of her abilities. She wasn't suited for the position and the performance of the whole department suffered. After dismissal, she was hired by another department, and I believe she's doing a fine job there. That validated my opinion of her abilities and proved my feeling that she could be a valuable employee in a position that suits her talents and skills better.

*or*

So far I haven't been in a position to hire or fire people, but there were cases when my colleagues were dismissed because of poor attitude and poor performance, which were affecting the whole section.

8   Are you satisfied with your department's and your company's performance in the last year or two?

*Whenever you talk about your former or current place of employment, don't use 'they', use 'we'. That way you project loyalty to your employer, despite the fact that you are looking for another job. The interviewer will be assured that once you join their team you are going to be loyal to them. Anyone who says 'they' isn't, psychologically, working for that company.*

A: Despite a harsh economic climate and widespread recession, the company maintained its position in the market, and even improved slightly. The introduction of enterprise bargaining and abolishment of restricted work practices resulted in improved overall efficiency and performance. The funds are still limited and more jobs are expected to go in the near future. Overall, our performance last year could be described as adequate.

# Interpersonal skills

## Adaptability

*It is the nature of a man as he grows older to protest against change, particularly change for the better.*

John Steinbeck

---

• Maintaining effectiveness and productivity in diverse environments and under influence of various positive or negative factors.
• Accepting new ideas, work practices, policies and procedures.
• Adapting to different people, their methods of communication, work practices and management style.

---

1 From your résumé I see that you have changed jobs several times over the past few years, and some of them were in the country. What problems have you had to face when moving?

A: I have always enjoyed meeting new people and going to new places. So far I have been able to recognize the opportunities and therefore gain valuable experience working for diversified companies in various parts of the country. Each move was different and none of them was easy, but the rewards and achievements always outweighed small inconveniences. My family shares my views and we haven't had any problems in moving house, making new friends, and adapting our lifestyle to suit local conditions.

2   Generally speaking, there are some differences between working in privately owned companies and working in government's departments. What do you think these differences are? Have you had any problems in adapting to one or the other?

*There are two possible answers. Which one you are going to use will depend on the employer that is interviewing you. Don't praise the private sector when interviewing for a job in a government department and vice versa. Whichever the case, tell them that differences aren't major ones and you haven't had any problems in adapting to different working environments.*

3   Give me an example of a situation when you had to adjust quickly to changes in priorities or in the organizational structure. What impact did the change have on you and how difficult was it to accept it?

*The best example here would be a situation when your boss was away and you performed his or her duties for a period of time. Mention that you had to learn new skills quickly in order to meet the demands of the job, adjust to different priorities, supervise your peers and still do most of your normal duties.*

4   How do you manage to attend interviews while still employed?

*The worst thing you could say is 'I told my employer I'm sick'. Your integrity would be damaged and you would lose many points for that.*

A:  I've taken a few days off from my annual leave, to give myself enough time to schedule and attend interviews. Due to my workload that wasn't easy and some overtime and weekend work will be necessary, but I'm used to working long hours. I try not to be absent from work for more than a few days at a time.

5   What are your feelings about working for a large company like ours?

*Nobody really likes large-scale organization; nobody likes to take orders from a superior who takes orders from a superior who takes orders …*

E.F. Schumacher, *Small is Beautiful*

*Beware of the hierarchy, bureaucracy and constraints of most big companies. In your answer, reflect on positive aspects and don't mention the negatives.*

A: I would welcome the opportunity to work in a large, reputable firm such as this. The strength, market position and resources of such a well-established organization are not available in smaller companies. That strong base presents a foundation for achievement and potential for advancement and diversification.

6  **What is your attitude towards working in a small company such as this one?**

*Big companies are small companies that succeeded.*

Robert Townsend, *Up The Organization*

A: Most innovative, energetic and highly competitive companies are not big in size. I have always highly valued the participation of employees in decision making and 'the family feeling' of a small company, where team spirit, daily challenges and hands-on involvement in solving business problems bring a sense of achievement and a quick response to changes and new opportunities.

## Assertiveness

- Having or showing confidence in oneself, belief and trust in one's own powers.
- Being firm and direct in conversation.
- The ability to stand up for one's beliefs and rights.

Most interviewers don't ask questions on assertiveness: the whole interview can give them a very good idea of how assertive you are. However, it is possible that you will be asked one of the following questions.

1  **Do you make your opinion known if your point of view differs from that of your superiors?**
*In the 'backside-covering' process, most of us voice our opinions if we don't share our superiors' ideas. If you agree to do something you don't want to be held liable for, you'd better tell them so. That way the responsibility will lie on someone else's shoulders. Use something along those lines, but don't mention any shedding of responsibility. The interviewer is testing your assertiveness and independence.*

*Tell him you always speak up and try to discuss issues with your boss so you can come up with a mutually acceptable solution.*

A: I always discuss issues and problems with my superiors. If my point of view differs from theirs, I put myself into their shoes and try to see their point of view. Then I explain my opinions to them. In that process we almost always find the right solution.

2 **If you had to characterize yourself in one sentence, what would you say?**

*Some interviewers like this sort of trap question. You have two options. Try to summarize your strongest points or offer a 'no-answer' reply.*

A: My main assets are the ability to communicate effectively and work individually or in a team, set goals and achieve them, and get the required jobs done (*good answer*).

*or*

Would you like to hire anybody who can characterize himself in one sentence? (*even better answer*).

3 **Give me an example of some of the most difficult one-to-one discussions or meetings you have had with your colleagues or subordinates.**

*A good example that could be used here is an occasion when you had to fire someone. If you have done that in the past, use it to score a few points by presenting yourself as considerate, tactful and compassionate, but also as a firm, no-nonsense decision maker and action taker.*

A: Some performance evaluation discussions, and especially termination discussions, were most difficult for me. Certain people find it very hard to assume responsibility and accountability for their actions, which calls for special skills in handling such meetings. I always try to see things from the other person's perspective, but I also make sure I make them understand my point of view by being firm and resisting the intimidation and bullying tactics some people use.

## Behavioural flexibility

- The ability to change and adjust views, methods used and behaviour to suit the particular situation or task.
- The capability to accept change around you.

1 Describe an occasion when, after your initial proposal or idea was rejected, you used a different approach and achieved your goal. What was the difference between the two approaches?

A: At my job with _____ (*the name of your employer*) one of my proposals for _____ (*purpose*) was rejected due to insufficiency of capital funds at the time. I didn't give up. My strategy was simple but effective. I clearly stated the problem we had, listed annual sums that had been wasted and calculated anticipated savings that my proposal would generate. I presented my request using graphs, charts and tables, and the management liked my new proposal and the whole idea!

2 Have you had any experience in supervising people with advanced degrees? Did you use a different approach to establish rapport with those individuals?

A: My job with _____ (*name a previous employer*) required supervision and co-ordination of technical staff, most of whom were engineers and scientists with higher degrees. It was a great opportunity for me to learn from those professionals, and the whole experience was very stimulating. I enjoy working with highly educated people. The most important aspects in building a rapport with them are mutual respect and an understanding of each other's needs and work philosophy. They have specific demands and need specific motivation and recognition for their work, of which they are very proud. Those traits require slightly different supervision methods.

3 How do you feel about a formal dress code in our department?

*Some companies have strict dress codes, such as a shirt, a tie and a jacket for men (no jeans or casuals) and a dress or skirt for women (no trousers). Tell them you would wear whatever is required by the code.*

A: The dress code in your department/company suits me. I have always liked to dress formally and feel very comfortable wearing a suit. I realize that a standard of dress is necessary for a company in this business in order to project a positive image to its customers and the general public.

4 How would you feel about working for a female supervisor?

A: I don't differentiate between people on the basis of their gender, the only thing that matters to me is their personality, efficiency and professionalism.

5 **Have you ever worked for a boss younger or less experienced than yourself?**

A: I haven't worked for such a boss. My former bosses were mostly very experienced professionals from whom I've learned a lot. In a sense, they were role models for me.

*or*

I have worked for a younger boss before. She was a good manager and motivator, we had a very productive relationship and we got along really well. I don't consider age as important as a person's credibility, professionalism and competence.

6 **How important to you is the aim to build relationships with clients, co-workers, peers or management?**

A: To me, interaction between people is the most important factor in any business. The ability to work together as a team, absolute honesty with peers and customers and mutual feelings of trust and understanding are essential for creating the efficient environment. A good team is always greater then the sum of the individual values of its members. A new dimension is created when people work harmoniously together.

7 **What types of people annoy you?**

A: People who annoy me are the ones who are not prepared to do their best and to contribute as team members. Unprofessional, unethical, dishonest people, gossipers and backstabbers are equally destructive and annoying. I find it hard to trust and rely on them. Usually, all such people are interested in is their pay cheque.

## Independence

- Taking action in your own hands.
- Resisting the influence of others.
- Making your views known.
- Being a self-starter, recognizing problems and taking actions to rectify them.
- The ability to work alone, with minimal supervision or without direct supervision.

1  **What kinds of decisions do you make independently in your present job? Give me some examples of those decisions.**

A:  In my job as _____, I'm responsible for all issues related to _____. Since I work alone most of the time, or as part of a small team, I have to make various kinds of decisions regularly and independently. For example, I decide _____.

2  **Tell me about an instance when you took matters into your own hands although it should have been handled by your superiors.**

*This is good opportunity to demonstrate your ability to successfully handle more complex problems and get the difficult jobs done. In addition to that, you can illustrate your initiative and tendency to assume higher responsibilities and take calculated risks.*

3  **Do you prefer working alone or being part of a team?**

*The answer to this question would have to be tailored to suit the nature of the job you are being interviewed for. No matter which style of work prevails on the job, don't forget to mention that you work effectively in any case.*

A:  Owing to the nature of my occupation and the kind of tasks that I encounter in my job, I have worked independently for a number of years. The broad range of my skills, my knowledge of the subject and my systematic and organized approach to work make me self-reliant and efficient in meeting the demands of this profession. I have also worked as part of a team where I had an opportunity to learn from others and improve my teamwork skills.

*or*

Although I have worked alone, I prefer team spirit and the interactions between team members while working towards a common goal. In a team people learn from each other and tend to achieve results faster, more efficiently and with greater satisfaction. The team approach to problem solving creates a homogeneous work force and more productive environment.

4  **Have you ever worked alone, without any supervision at all?**

*Most people have worked without direct supervision or any supervision at all. Exploit the fact that you successfully completed the tasks given to you and that you didn't need any help or assistance. Mention your systematic approach to problem solving, the use of experience gained in similar situations and the ability to identify and rectify problems.*

A:  I have worked without supervision for prolonged periods of time. As a self-starter I can identify problems, devise a plan of action and assume full responsibility for my activities and the successful completion of required tasks.

5   **Do you consider yourself to be a self-starter?**

A:  I do. I never rely on someone else to take the initiative; I take the initiative myself. My education and experience mean that I am able to recognize potential problems and areas critical for the successful accomplishment of projects. Trend watching and looking for the clues are important in the process.

6   **What do you do in your job that is not covered by your job description? Why do you do that type of work?**

A:  To achieve goals and produce results I sometimes choose to perform various tasks that are not, strictly speaking, a part of it. Modern work practices and a competitive climate call for more flexibility and a broader range of skills. By doing more than required not only do I learn more but I also become more efficient and productive. If I'm able to do the task, instead of waiting for the job to be done, I simply go for it.

7   **Have you ever felt the company's constraints on you and have you ever had to go against those traditions and policies to reach your goal?**

*Similar to question 2 on page 110. It's a 'Catch-22' situation: by displaying your initiative and independence you go against the rules; if you always play by the rules you will not be seen as innovative. Of the two evils choose the lesser one.*

A:  We all feel the constraints of some policies and procedures from time to time. However, to achieve uniformity and consistency and to ensure that relevant standards and regulations are followed it is necessary to have those policies and procedures in place. It is always possible to 'cut corners' and achieve the required results sooner or with less effort, but I have never taken the path of least resistance.

## Negotiation skills

1   **Have you had experience in negotiating big deals with suppliers? What have you achieved as the outcome of those negotiations?**

A: My experience in negotiation helped me get some very good deals on spare parts and equipment for projects. I have established very good and professional relationships with vendors and suppliers, so getting the best price possible was a natural outcome of my efforts. On average, I achieved savings between ten and twenty per cent on listed wholesale prices, and in some cases discounts were as high as forty per cent. Some vendors and retailers are very keen to establish a business with big companies and subsequent price reductions could be significant.

2   **Tell me about an instance when you had to negotiate with union officials about an issue that could not be resolved 'by the book'.**

A: In one instance I was involved in negotiations regarding the use of _____ (*mention the situation from your experience*). It was a specific issue and union officials were not keen to accept the changes, but after long and hard negotiations they agreed and the changes were implemented successfully.

3   **When you applied for your previous jobs, did you negotiate your salary or did you simply accept the figures determined by your employer?**

*Apart from evaluating your negotiation skills this question probes into a sensitive area of salary negotiations. Whatever you say may be used against you when the time comes for a talk about money. So use extreme caution here!*

A: Because of my education, knowledge and relevant professional experience, I have always been able to negotiate better terms of employment with employers, who realized that money-saving measures do not attract high-calibre candidates, and that additional money conceded would be the best investment possible – the investment in the right person for the job!

4   **Have you ever had to negotiate terms of a contract with a customer in order to get a sale? What concessions did you make and what was the outcome?**

A: In today's buyer's market it is sometimes necessary to negotiate the price of a contract or some of the terms in order to get a sale. I have had a few cases of that kind. Although I made a few small concessions in response to a customer's growing demands, I managed to change other aspects of those contracts. Those gains brought additional revenue from the customers, without them realizing it.

Tough negotiation is not always the best approach to securing deals. Sometimes 'don't change the price, change the package' tactics work much better.

## Sales ability/persuasiveness

*Two shoe salesmen find themselves in a rustic, backward part of Africa. The first salesman wires back to his head office: 'There is no prospect of sales. No one wears shoes here'. The other salesman wires: 'No one wears shoes here. We can dominate the market. Send all possible stock'.*

William Davis, *The Innovators*

1   **What are the best ideas/suggestions/proposals you made to your boss? How successful were they?**
*When answering this question, select an instance when your proposal was accepted. Make sure you outline the benefits to your employer that resulted from your contributions.*

2   **Explain briefly your attitude and approach to selling, either products or ideas. What methods do you use and why?**

A:  My whole approach to selling is based on the fact that whenever we want to get co-operation from people, persuade them to buy something or win an argument, we have to speak in the other person's terms. For example, instead of urging customers to buy equipment or products that I think they need, I encourage them to give me their ideas. That way customers feel they are coming up with ideas, creating the designs and making decisions. Once I succeed in doing this, I don't have to sell. They buy.

3   **Describe your most satisfying experience in gaining management support for your idea or proposal.**
*This question requires a specific example from your past experience. Select an instance when you achieved savings, increased profits, improved safety or work practices or initiated something significant.*

A:  Based on my experience in logistics, warehouse management and stock control, I devised a programme for reducing the number of spare parts kept on the shelf and better stock management. The programme was relatively easy to implement and resulted in considerable savings. The management welcomed the idea and recognized my efforts by promoting me to the position of Warehouse Supervisor.

4   **What was your most disappointing experience in attempting to persuade your superiors to accept your views?**

A:  My opinions and views are generally highly regarded and sought after by management, due to my knowledge of the job and relevant experience. There have been, however, a couple of occasions when decisions were made despite my strong objections. In one instance, some major earthmoving equipment was overdue for a major service, but it was decided to postpone the service for a considerable period. The equipment failed catastrophically, as I predicted, and expenses were high.

5   **What do your subordinates think your strengths and weaknesses are? How do you know they would respond that way?**

A:  It's a bit difficult to predict their response to this question. Judging by my successful and professional relationship with them, I would expect to be portrayed as fair and firm leader, good communicator and a person of high integrity and morale. I have always been able to motivate them, even when times were tough and tasks demanding.

## Communication, negotiation and persuasion skills

1   **How do you assure your subordinates and co-workers that you are listening to what they say?**

A:  When I make a decision or take an action that involves my co-workers or subordinates, I always make sure I get their input. It is important to adapt to different personality styles and get constant feedback in order to avoid conflicts, misunderstandings or bad feelings. The doors of my office are open to people with constructive suggestions, work-related problems and genuine enquiries.

2   **Have you ever misinterpreted any instruction, message or information? What were the outcomes of those situations?**

A:  I always devote my exclusive attention to the person speaking to me. That way most misunderstandings can be eliminated and effective communication established. I notice that most poor listeners, when they are not talking, are busy rehearsing what they are going to say next. That makes it very difficult to exchange ideas and messages.

**3  Have you ever done any public speaking or presentations?**

A: The nature of my profession means that presentations, meetings and conferences play a very prominent role in my day-to-day activities. As part of _____ (*an award, restructuring, a company's ongoing educational policy, etc.*) I run a few training courses for _____ (*tradesmen, clerical staff, trainees …*). So far I have successfully participated in various seminars, presentations and conferences and delivered speeches on a range of _____ (*technical, managerial, scientific …*) topics.

**4  What were some of the biggest or most demanding groups/audiences you made presentations to?**

A: Last year I participated in _____ (*The Third International Conference on Molecular Biology, Electrical Energy Symposium, etc.*). My research paper was published and I was one of the speakers. The participants and guests were very prominent people specializing in that area. Judging by the number of questions I had to answer after the speech, my presentation was well received.

**5  Have you ever written any procedures, specifications, policies, tenders or similar documents for use by a client or your own firm?**

A: Writing equipment specifications/tenders/operational procedures is a vital part of my role as _____ (*job title*). That kind of technical document ensures that the equipment and services provided by my company meet all relevant standards and any additional, predetermined criteria. Likewise, any contract, service or equipment provided by vendors has to comply with our specifications and internal standards.

**6  What types of written proposals or reports have you done?**

A: My present position includes writing (*give details*) reports and proposals. Each of the document types mentioned requires a different approach and makes use of different writing techniques to suit its structure and to convey the message in the most effective way.

**7  What were some of your most difficult writing assignments?**

A: I have written quite a few important and very demanding assignments, but the most challenging one was my _____ (*Diploma/Masters/PhD thesis*). The hard work and time invested in its preparation paid off, for it received very favourable reviews and was awarded the highest distinction.

8   Have you ever had to write technical/training manuals for
    _____ (tradespeople, plant operators, catering staff,
    etc.)?

A:  So far I haven't been involved in that type of activity, but part
    of my duties is to _____ (*regularly revise and update
    operating procedures, produce short instructions to line
    people, implement communication plans and strategies ...*). I
    feel confident in my technical writing abilities and if this job
    requires me to, it shouldn't take me long to produce quality
    documents.

    *or*

    Whilst with _____ (*company*), I produced a
    comprehensive training manual for on-the-job training of
    _____ (*sales staff, crane operators, nurses, boiler
    makers ...*). I also wrote a few chapters in the company's
    Internal Procedures Manual.

9   What are the most important documents/proposals/reports
    you have ever written?

A:  Most of my business proposals and tenders were successful,
    even at times of recession and in the toughest sectors of the
    market, but the _____ (*$400,000, £1 million ...*) tender
    for _____ (*project*) made the most significant
    contribution to my employer's profitability in the past year.
    I devoted a great deal of my energy and experience to that
    deal. My efforts were recognized and that gave me the
    greatest sense of achievement in my job at _____
    (*company name*).

10  Do you have any rules that you follow when writing
    reports/proposals? What are they? How do you implement
    them? Why are they important?

    *This is a typical example of multiple questions asked
    together. Make sure you remember all of them. If you don't,
    ask the interviewer to repeat the question(s). You don't have
    to answer them as they were separate questions, but reflect
    on each one of them in your answer.*

A:  There are some basic rules that have to be followed in
    writing. First we have to determine what type of audience
    will read our written message, which will have an impact on
    the style and document format used. Secondly, we have to
    establish the purpose of the written assignment: what is the
    message? The next question to be considered is what
    aspects/points/details should be emphasized in order to
    achieve effective, clear and comprehensive communication.

Finally we come to the actual contents of our written document. It should always include the three essential parts: an introduction, a body and a conclusion. That format is usually the most effective way to get the message and information to the readers.

11 **Please tell me about an instance when you managed to convince or influence others or when you got co-operation from others and won them over to your way of thinking.**

To answer this convoluted question you may use an example from home, with your spouse, children, parents, relatives, or friends, but a better choice would be an example from your working life, involving your boss, colleagues, clients or people working for you. Some of the issues you could mention may be:

• The approach you used.
• How you chose your words.
• When you approached them (how you timed your actions).
• What you achieved.

## Management ability

Be prepared for some 'theoretical' questions here. Although most interviewers look for specific, action or problem-oriented answers, and ask exact and precise questions to elicit such answers, some of them like broad general questions. The candidate's answers to these questions reveal a lot, not only what they say and are prepared to say, but also what they don't want to, or cannot, say! So, take a few hours to think about general topics such as management, the role of people in organizations, motivation, effective communication methods and so on. It will help you express your views and better understand the interviewer's. Some of the typical questions of a general nature are:

1 How would you define your management philosophy?
2 What do you think good management is?
3 What is your human resources philosophy? How would you define the role of people in the organization?

# Control

*Ready? Shoot! Aim!*

Japanese view of Western management techniques

1  **Describe a particularly difficult management situation you have encountered, how you approached the problem and the outcome of the whole situation.**

   *Don't forget that the control methods you use and your control skills are being evaluated here. The core of your message should be that you were in control of events and people, not vice versa.*

2  **What methods do you use to predict the future workload for your staff?**

A: The departmental monthly and yearly plans are the base for predictions of that kind. Most major activities are scheduled (except major breakdowns and equipment failures) and regularly updated and revised. Another important aspect of this planning process is previous experience and knowledge of the department and most factors that could affect the smooth running of the business. (*Now add some specific methods that you use or are planning to use.*)

The next two questions will not have listed answers. Many books have been written on subjects like Management By Objectives (MBO) and Total Quality Control (TQC). More and more managers are using these methods and the chances that you will be asked this type of question are increasing. However, opinions differ, although the positive ones are prevalent. In your answers (if you have had experience with the methods mentioned) concentrate on the benefits achieved. If you haven't had such experience, tell them you are familiar with the concepts and that you are considering implementing them. Then give reasons for your decisions or opinion regarding the effectiveness of advanced management methods.

3  **Do you use Management By Objectives? How would you evaluate its effectiveness?**

4  **Are you familiar with Total Quality Control concepts? Have you ever used or implemented TQC in your area of responsibility?**

## Delegation

Make sure that you emphasize the fact that when you delegate tasks, you still hold the responsibility for the job being well done. Employers don't like people who shed or delegate their responsibility and accountability.

**1   Have you ever delegated responsibility?**

**A:**  I make delegating tasks and responsibilities my constant goal. If you expect people to develop their skills and abilities, you have to give them responsibility. My method is to tell them what the objectives of a certain task are, what criteria will be used to evaluate their performance and then let them do it. I make myself available to help them along the way and to monitor their progress.

**2   What type of assignments do you delegate to your subordinates?**

**A:**  When I delegate some task or assign responsibility to a person, I have a very good idea of their capabilities, strengths and weaknesses. To challenge and motivate people, I try to assign them tasks which are slightly above their current level of expertise. That way they keep learning and growing on the job. Sometimes it takes them a little longer to complete the assignments, but the benefits of this approach are far greater than the drawbacks.

**3   What steps do you take in delegating?**

**A:**  First, I tell the person what I expect them to accomplish, second, I set the standards they are expected to reach and third, I keep monitoring their progress and helping them if necessary. I make it a priority to make sure the employee knows how to handle a task and how to accomplish the goal.

**4   Have you ever made a mistake in delegating? Tell me about the outcome and what caused that mistake.**

**A:**  I couldn't say I have made mistakes in delegating, but I had some temporary setbacks when I delegated tasks that were far above the capabilities of my subordinates. The initial results were not as good as they could had been, but in the long run the benefits were obvious, for my subordinates acquired new skills and mastered demanding tasks. Initially, when I started the job, I wasn't delegating enough, mostly because I didn't know my workers well. Once I learned their capabilities, I gained confidence in them and became successful in delegating. That's what delegating is all about: confidence in people.

5   **How do you keep track of assignments made to subordinates?**

A:  I use a simple but effective computerized filing system. Each employee has an individual database file with all planned activities, estimated time and information on progress and results achieved. That way I know what each person is doing at any time.

6   **Do you sometimes feel that to get a job done properly you have to do it yourself?**

A:  People who feel that way don't have trust in their co-workers and subordinates, and probably don't know how to delegate properly. By knowing my people, their skills, abilities and personalities, I have been able to successfully delegate tasks and improve their skills.

7   **What kinds of decisions do you reserve for yourself? Why don't you delegate them to others?**

A:  An effective manager doesn't delegate *all* his work. Some tasks are too complex, too urgent or too important to be delegated. A manager should attend to those issues himself. Whenever a decision directly affects _____ (*people in my department, company's profitability, legal issues, efficiency* ...) I make that decision and assume responsibility.

## Developing subordinates

1   **Have you ever been involved in hiring employees?**

A:  So far I haven't been in a position to make decisions on hiring, but I have been involved in the evaluation of applicants and in making recommendations and giving expert advice on suitability and technical knowledge of candidates.

*or*

As a _____ (*supervisor, departmental manager* ...) I have interviewed candidates for various positions within the company. Either individually or as a member of a recruiting panel, I have been involved in selection and hiring of the best applicants.

**2   How do you help your subordinates to improve their performance?**

A:  In my opinion, the best motivator and the best help in the learning process is personal attention. I always make myself available to people by creating a supportive and productive atmosphere which will encourage them to learn, improve and expand their views. That sort of atmosphere helps them build confidence in themselves, in the company and in their manager.

**3   What is your opinion on the importance of training and development?**

A:  In today's rapidly changing business climate, effective training is absolutely necessary to improve the efficiency and readiness of the work force. However, training is not just about developing skills. It is an instrument for attaining the company's objectives, such as innovation, creative thinking, workers' participation in decision making and total quality control. Training and development is about human resources and their role in a productive environment.

**4   What are the major training and development needs of the people in your department?**

A:  The training needs in my department vary between certain groups of people and between individuals (*give details*). Also, there is training in supervision and management methods for senior professionals, supervisors and managers. Some members of our team are currently studying for postgraduate degrees.

**5   What management methods and techniques do you use in developing your staff?**

A:  In the area of human resource developments, I have initiated and put into practice a few programmes. Our annual performance review analyses accomplishments and areas for improvement, and serves as a basis for determining the skills that each employee is lacking. The human resources review, which also takes place once a year, outlines the specific steps employees should take to improve their skills and acquire new knowledge. Last, but not least, through daily contacts with my subordinates, I keep aware of their talents, strengths and weaknesses, and ask for their views on their own training and development needs.

6  **What is your attitude towards human resources philosophy and the role of people in today's organizations?**

A:  It sounds like a cliché, but people are the company's most important asset. It can't be seen directly on balance sheets and annual reports, but people are the key to peak performance and, subsequently, business success. In today's work force, which is better educated and more skilled than ever before, the task of every manager and supervisor is to establish communication channels, allow free flow of information and implement the programmes and policies that will motivate people, prepare them for challenges and give them job satisfaction, which is perceived as increasingly important for creating the right business climate.

## Leadership

*To lead people, walk behind them.*

Lao-tzu

The Western world has been suffering from a chronic lack of leaders for some time. Many companies suffer from that illness too. These days, most employees are administered. They are treated as numbers, not people. Rules and regulations don't leave much room for leadership. Policies are inflexible and companies apply them across the board. In such a climate it is very difficult to nurture leadership. Leadership is closely associated with innovation, vision and trust. Sadly, you won't find too much of that in many of today's organizations. However, some employers value leadership more than others and it is likely that they will ask you one or more of the following questions to assess your leadership abilities.

1  **Do you think you are a smart person?**

A:  To me, smart people are not necessarily the ones with high IQs or degrees. Education and intelligence are the ability to meet life's situations and perform on the job to the best of one's abilities. We show our value by the way we deal with people, approach business problems and make decisions. With that in mind, and without any false modesty, I would consider myself a smart person. Of course, there are many things I don't know, but I make constant learning and self-improvement my main goal. To me, to be smart means to ask questions, listen to what people say, apply knowledge and know-how to problems and learn from my own, and preferably from other people's, mistakes.

**2  Do you like working with people?**

*The ability to be a contributing member of a team by dealing successfully with people from various backgrounds is viewed as essential by employers.*

A:  I have always enjoyed teamwork and interaction with my co-workers and customers. In today's very competitive and highly specialized business environment, it is of paramount importance to organize and co-ordinate the efforts of many people to achieve goals and sustain growth. Although I consider my ability to work well with people, to motivate them and communicate with them effectively one of my most important assets, I constantly try to keep improving those skills.

**3  How do you show interest in and keep in contact with your co-workers?**

A:  The key to successful people handling lies in knowing them. So I make sure I have a good idea about what my co-workers want, their feelings and what they expect from me. Showing them what my ideas can do for them makes them more receptive and co-operative. I show interest through regular meetings, discussions and consultations, and through becoming genuinely interested in their work and achievements.

**4  In your opinion, what makes a good manager?**

A:  Good managers are people dedicated to company goals and policies, people who know how to manage employees, motivate them and develop them to their fullest potential. The good manager creates the right kind of environment by stimulating the desire to excel in employees, delegates responsibility and promotes teamwork.

**5  What specifically do you do to set an example for your subordinates/co-workers?**

A:  My personal credo is not to ask anything from my subordinates that I, as manager, wouldn't ask from myself. To be fair and just, to treat people with respect and to be genuinely interested in them are the secrets of my success with people. I consider creating the right work environment my most important task, and to achieve that I have to start with myself, by setting the right example for my staff.

6 **What was the most difficult group you have had to co-operate with? Why was dealing with them difficult?**

*The answer to this question will depend on your particular occupation and experience. You can relate to a problem with a demanding, unprofessional, unethical, unmotivated, abusive or unco-operative client, another department, work group, contractor or any other group you had a problem dealing with. Whichever example you use, make sure you emphasize the steps you took to rectify the problem, your efforts and willingness to resolve the issue. A good example would be handling an industrial dispute or strike (after it happened) or discussions and negotiations with workers and union officials in order to prevent it from happening. Companies with strong anti-union sentiments would love your tough approach and loyalty to your employer.*

7 **Do you have any staff that do not work together well? What have you done to rectify the problem?**

**A:** Most of my staff work together very well and have strong feelings of belonging to the team. Occasionally, there are misunderstandings and disputes that have to be resolved, but these are more of an exception than a rule. My task in such cases is to act as a mediator, bringing people together and openly discussing the issues. It is very important for me to preserve neutrality in those circumstances, maintain integrity and project sincerity.

8 **How would you define the difference between management and leadership?**

**A:** It isn't easy to define leadership. I see it as one of the managerial activities, the one which improves productivity by stimulating creativity, improving morale and personal satisfaction, influencing workers and redirecting their behaviour to satisfy a wide range of objectives. Management, on the other hand, is about controlling the company's resources, making decisions that will increase efficiency and profitability, improve working conditions and safety, and create a stable, reliable and motivated work force. Managers' tasks are to make sure that company policies and procedures are adhered to, and to plan and control the various activities that have to lead to desired results. To me, management is the issue of ability and controlling, while leadership is about trust, credibility and vision.

9  Do you consider yourself a better manager or a better leader? What are the reasons for that?

A:  To be a good manager, one has to be familiar with the company rules and policies, various legal issues, business methods and strategies and planning and controlling process. Good leaders don't necessarily have those traits. Their biggest strength is their ability to lead and motivate people. They enjoy almost unquestioned support from their followers. So far I have been able to achieve balance between those qualities, to be successful in a management process and to motivate people to achieve better results.

10  How would you describe your job as a supervisor?

A:  The effective supervisor must perform certain functions to enable his team to carry out its tasks. He has to define tasks to be done, make a plan of how to achieve those tasks, allocate work and resources to individuals, control quality of work done and progression of jobs, constantly assess the performance against the plan and developed criteria and adjust the plan, if necessary, to reflect the changes and modifications. The supervisor also has to create an environment that will support the efforts of his team and make people more receptive to ideas, enthusiastic about their work, loyal to their supervisor and the company and committed to the company's goals.

## Planning, organizing and time management

*Work expands so as to fill the time available for its completion.*

C. Northcote Parkinson, *Parkinson's Law*

1  What methods do you use in scheduling your time and setting priorities?

A:  I regard planning as an important tool in managing my work and achieving first-class results. I plan my time on daily, weekly, monthly and six-monthly bases. Software packages for scheduling and project management help me in adjusting my plans and scheduling activities. These plans are the basis for daily 'to do' lists. Every evening I list issues and tasks to be performed the next day and assign priorities to them. My experience in carrying out the tasks of my job helps me determine those priorities.

2   **What action do you take when your plans and schedules are upset by unforeseen circumstances?**

A:  A good plan, be it daily, weekly, monthly or longer range, should always leave some room for unforeseen circumstances, problems or developments that are difficult or impossible to predict. When I plan or schedule activities, I try to build in a degree of flexibility and adaptability, so changes and rearrangements can be made quickly and easily, with minimum delays or interruptions of any kind. A reasonable contingency factor is imperative in uncertain or unstable times and some activities.

3   **What were your last year's objectives? Have you achieved them?**

*When talking about your plans and objectives, state not only what was planned but also why, and how the plan was realized.*

4   **How do you plan your day-to-day activities?**

A:  My first job every morning is to go through my 'to do' list (created the day before, or during my previous weekly planning exercise), revise it and set priorities. Some jobs may be urgent and important, some may be important but not urgent and vice versa. To avoid procrastination I first attend to the tasks I dread most. Once I finish those tasks I feel much more confident and efficient, because I know that the most difficult or awkward tasks have been accomplished.

5   **Who schedules your sales trips? How do you decide which clients to see and when?**

*Ideally, you should schedule your own trips. By telling them that, you project an image of an independent and organized decision maker.*

A:  My monthly, six-monthly and yearly plans serve as a basis for scheduling trips. Every now and then they have to be changed due to various developments, such as the start of a new project, major upgrades of plant and equipment, unplanned purchases and changes in client's personnel. All those events call for earlier visits and further building of business relationships. I make most decisions and plans myself, which then get an approval from the sales manager.

**6 How do you familiarize yourself with the latest developments in your company after being away for a few days?**

A: When I'm away on business, I keep in touch with my superiors and my colleagues. Daily telephone contacts are very important for the smooth operation of the business. When I return, I spend a few minutes with each of the people I work with and review the developments that took place while I was away.

**7 Do you have a work backlog in your department? What factors caused that backlog?**

*Never admit that you are the cause of the backlog. Even if you recognize the existence of a backlog in your department, you can emphasize that your projects/jobs/task are being done on time or ahead of schedule. Underline the importance of your planning techniques.*

**8 Do you use any software packages for project management? Why did you choose that particular program?**

A: I am familiar with a few project management programs, such as_____ (*Timeline, Project Manager Workbench, Harvard Project Manager, Microsoft Project* ...). I prefer _____ , because of its capabilities and user friendliness. The manuals are comprehensive and well written and the technical support is outstanding.

**9 How do you keep a record of items and issues that require your attention? How do you prioritize them?**

A: I consider record keeping an important management tool. I use a diary to record all issues and events, as well as the whiteboard, for issues that I have to be aware of constantly. I also use daily 'to do' lists and 'people to see or call' lists which help me to organize and plan my time. A few levels of priority are assigned to various tasks and issues. Some of them may be important and urgent, urgent but not important, important but not urgent, and so on. Each priority reflects these criteria: importance and urgency.

**10 Describe a typical day on your job (if the candidate is employed).**

*or*

**Describe a typical day on your last job (for unemployed).**

*Amongst other things, your skills in planning and organizing your time, prioritizing and scheduling your duties and managing your resources are evaluated by this question. Efficiency, effective time management and organized approach to activities can help you frame your answer.*

11 Do you consider yourself a future-, present- or past-oriented person?

A: I try to live in the present, thinking in terms of what needs to be done now, instead of thinking about the past or worrying about the future. Past experiences are always valuable, and making plans for the future is an important business activity, but I concentrate my efforts on current problems and issues.

## Staff co-ordination

1 What performance appraisal procedure and technique do you use for evaluating your subordinates?

A: We have a formal six-monthly performance evaluation programme, in the form of one-on-one discussions between the manager and each staff member. There are detailed evaluation criteria that address attendance record, quality of work, ideas and suggestions made, training and development, achievement of goals and targets set on previous sessions, and so on. In addition to these formal evaluations, I use every opportunity to praise my staff for their efforts and recognize a job well done, or, if necessary, to reprimand them for poor performance, discipline problems, or any serious breach of regulations or company policy.

2 How do you establish rapport with your staff and peers?

A: To me, establishing rapport seems to be a natural tendency. The greatest part is often established non-verbally. By being empathetic, treating people with respect and being willing to listen and help, I create a feeling of trust and confidence in my staff. Matching our behaviour to suit the particular situation or person also helps in a process. Matching voice tone or tempo to that of the person I'm talking to, controlling my body language, posture and gesture is also important. All that is done almost automatically, naturally. I consider myself lucky for not having any problems in establishing rapport with my peers, superiors or staff.

**3 Describe the basic form and content of your staff meetings.**

A: Our daily meetings are very brief. They cover major tasks to be performed during the day, current developments and actualities. Weekly meetings communicate information from management and other departments, and include a planning session for the coming week. Each staff member gets a chance to contribute by informing others on his or her projects and activities, or by raising various issues or concerns. The chair of the meeting changes on a rotational basis. The manager acts as a mediator, moderator and co-ordinator.

**4 To what extent do your subordinates participate in the decisions you make?**

A: Whenever appropriate I ask for input from my colleagues and subordinates, as either an opinion or a recommendation. Involving them in the decision-making process makes them feel active participants, not just passive bystanders. It also prepares them for more senior positions in the future. In some cases, team members make their own decisions and assume responsibility for the successful completion of a task.

**5 Can you tell me about an instance when an employee came to you with a personal problem? How did you handle that situation?**

A: I can recall quite a few of those instances. On one occasion, I noticed decreased productivity of one of my employees. The person I'm talking about was one of the best and most reliable workers, yet her performance was suffering for some reason. Just when I planned to talk to her, she came to see me and explained her problem. Her father was seriously ill and she asked me for a few days off, because she had used her annual leave a few months before. I checked the validity of her claims and approved ten days of paid leave on compassionate grounds. Everything ended well, her father recovered and she is still one of the best performers, more committed than ever.

**6 What actions do you take if a subordinate is not performing on the job?**

A: The first step in coaching a failing employee is to determine the causes for failure, such as lack of talent, lack of motivation or interest, inexperience, inadequate resources or time, personal problems and so on. Once the reason is established, a confidential counselling session will have to produce clear guidelines for improvement in the future, with specific tasks, targets and time frames. The manager's point of view has to be clearly stated to the employee, as well as the performance criteria. The next stage would involve careful monitoring of the employee and giving specific feedback on his or her efforts and actions.

7   **How would you dismiss an employee who is not performing adequately?**

A:   If, after two or more counselling sessions and simultaneous continuous performance monitoring, an employee fails to improve, dismissal is probably the only option. It is in the best interests of the company to deal with non-productive people this way. In the termination discussion, all necessary points have to be clarified and discussed, such as factual evidence of inadequate results, contributing factors, key reasons for dismissal and detailed conditions of the termination of contract or transfer. In some cases, when the employee has a history of accomplishments and could make a contribution to the company in a different position, a transfer is a viable option. All applicable company rules and procedures should be followed, as well as any laws and regulations that govern this particular situation. All actions and conclusions would have to be well documented and the dismissed employee informed of all benefits and aids available (termination payment, personnel office help, placement agencies, and so on).

# Professional knowledge

*An expert is one who knows more and more about less and less.*

Nicholas Murray Butler

It is very difficult, almost impossible, to list, let alone answer, the specific questions of a technical or highly specialized nature that interviewers may ask you. The questions will depend entirely on your occupation, interviewer's knowledge of that area and the type of job you will be interviewed for. The primary purpose of this section is to give you an idea of the format and content of specialized questions. Even the questions given here are broad in content. Be prepared for very specific ones, such as: 'On the automation project mentioned, what brand of programmable logic controllers did you use and what software and graphic package did you install?'

1   Have you had any experience in family law (lawyer)/high-voltage switching (electrical engineer)/AutoCAD or computer drafting? (Draftsman)

2   Your résumé states that you organized plant shutdowns and major periodical maintenance. How did you approach the whole process and what planning and monitoring methods did you use? (Maintenance Planner)

3   Give me an example of an industrial dispute that you handled recently. (Industrial Relations Officer)

4   One of your achievements at ACME Company was the introduction of the MBO (Management by Objectives) technique. Could you briefly explain the reasons for that decision, the difficulties that you faced and name some benefits that resulted from that step?(Department Manager)

5   Tell me about an instance when you had to dismiss an employee who was not performing adequately. (Personnel Officer)

6   How do you prepare yourself for a particularly difficult and important sales presentation? (Sales Representative)

7   Every now and then we have the difficult task of establishing rapport with a particular child or the whole group. Tell me about some of your experiences. What methods do you normally use to solve that type of problem? (Teacher)

8   Have you ever worked with UNIX and what programming languages did you use? (Computer Programmer)

9   Have you ever treated patients suffering from Parkinson's disease? (Medical Practitioner)

## Self-development

*The only things worth learning are the things you learn after you know it all.*

Harry S. Truman

1   How do you keep informed about the developments and news in other departments or sectors of your company?

A:  I regularly attend departmental meetings and read the company's newsletter, which helps me stay attuned to current trends and developments. However, I gather most valuable information from my dealings with my colleagues in other sections and departments. Quite often we work together on multi-disciplinary projects. That kind of interaction is very important, because it helps to promote understanding and appreciation of other people's jobs and encourages teamwork.

**2   Are you subscribed to any trade or professional magazines? Which ones?**

**A:**  I receive quite a few professional journals, but some of them are particularly useful. I have been receiving _____ (*name of journal*) for almost four years now.

**3   What are your current/future plans for self-improvement?**

**A:**  My general goal is to keep learning, expanding my knowledge and improving my skills. Technology has been changing so rapidly that in order to keep pace with the change one has to make constant self-improvement a top priority. Some of my education will be informal, through reading and on-the-job learning. I also plan to take courses in _____ (*relevant course*) at _____ (*institution*).

**4   What are some of the areas in which you would like to improve in future? Mention some area not directly related to your work, something 'nice to have' rather than 'absolute necessity' for the job.**

**A:**  Although my performance appraisals have been extremely positive, I would like to improve my (*book-keeping, computer, management* ...) skills. I find that area very important for my professional growth and my contribution to my employer.

**5   What have you accomplished in the line of self-improvement during the last year or two?**

**A:**  Six months ago I _____ (*obtained my bachelor's degree, started my studies towards a Master's degree* ...). I also attended a few _____ (*recognized, university accredited, informal* ...) courses/workshops/seminars. They helped me improve my _____ (*management skills, typing skills* ...). I also received extensive on-the-job training that helped me in getting promoted to _____ (*shift supervisor, electrical inspector, senior analyst* ...).

**6   Have you attended/participated in any professional seminars/conferences in the past year or two?**

**A:**  I recently published a paper and presented it at _____ (name conference or symposium). I also attended _____ (*meeting/conference/seminar*).

7  Were they company sponsored or did you do it at your own initiative and expense?

A:  Some of the courses, mostly internal ones, were sponsored by the company. I attended most of the external courses and conferences at my own expense. I regard that training as a valuable investment and an effective way to improve my skills and performance at work.

8  How do you see your present position changing over the next couple of years? What are you doing to prepare yourself for the changes ahead?

*The answer to the first question will depend on your particular situation. In the second part of your answer outline your plans for self-development and improvement or broadening of your skills.*

# Decision making

## Decisiveness

1  What kinds of decisions do you tend to make faster and for which ones do you need more time?

*In your answer, emphasize the fact that you generally make decisions quickly and stick to them, changing them slowly (only if necessary). These are the traits of successful people. You can use the answers for questions 2 and 3 to expand on this.*

2  Tell me about the most difficult decisions you have made recently. Why were they difficult?

A:  The most difficult decisions I made were the ones that either directly affected other people or had a big impact on my employer's success and profitability. One of the toughest ones was the decision to use contract labour for large projects and major maintenance work. I made that decision with higher efficiency, reliability and profitability in mind. On the other side were restricted work practices, high wages and overtime penalties and low morale and effectiveness of the permanent work force. That strategy meant a number of redundancies through retirements and lay-offs, but the bottom line is always the business itself. It has to survive, or a much higher number of people would be affected. Tough times do call for tough measures.

3    Have you ever delayed a decision to give you more time to
     think? What was the outcome of that decision?

A:   There is always some vital information or fact that has to be
     known in order to make the right decision. If that
     information is not available and if delaying the decision
     would not have an impact on the results, I usually postpone
     making a decision until those critical pieces are put in the
     place. That is my main reason for occasional delay in
     making a decision. Very rarely I need time to think about a
     problem. I make decisions fairly quickly and change them
     slowly, only if I see that the anticipated results could not be
     achieved that way.

## Judgement

1    What are some of the most important decisions you have
     made in your life?

     *In your answer use examples such as a decision to migrate
     to another country, to change career or move from town to
     town, to acquire a second degree or a postgraduate
     qualification, to join the army, or anything as significant as
     that.*

2    In your job, what decisions take you longest to reach?
     *Similar to question 1 under 'Decisiveness'.*

3    Can you give me some examples of good and not-so-good
     decisions you have made recently?

     *When you mention some of the bad decisions you have
     made (as few as possible), quickly point out what corrective
     action you took and talk about the eventual successful
     outcome.*

A:   I always feel it's better to take a calculated risk, to stand up
     and make a decision, even if it's the wrong one, than not to
     make a decision at all. Problems cannot be solved by not
     taking action and by not making decisions.

4    What do you do when you have an important decision to
     make?

A:   Before making an important decision, I take three basic
     steps. First, I analyse all aspects of the issue and all possible
     consequences. Second, I try to anticipate potential problems
     that can affect or be caused by my decision. Third, I talk to
     people who would be affected by that decision and get their
     input. By following these rules I make sure that I choose the
     optimal option and make the right decision.

## Problem solving

1  Have you ever recognized or noticed a particular problem before your colleagues or superiors?

*Emphasize the fact that you always keep your eyes and ears open. You continuously analyse trends and have the ability to notice problems at a very early stage. Employers like this kind of attitude.*

A: On some occasions I noticed certain problems with a potentially serious impact on _____ (*production, safety, morale, efficiency* …). Familiarity with equipment and procedures is an important part of my job. It enables me to recognize and identify trends, patterns, potential problems and critical success factors at an early stage, usually earlier than others could notice them. (*Now add an example from your experience.*)

2  How do you prepare yourself for potential problems?

A: I always try to look at a problem as if for the first time. I don't bind myself to the ways the same or similar problem was handled in the past. I don't assume anything and take nothing for granted. The only thing I know from the beginning is that the solution is there: I just have to find it.

3  What problems that you are currently trying to solve came as a surprise to you? Was it possible to anticipate the occurrence of those problems?

A: This is where know-how comes in. It isn't just expert knowledge mixed with the right kind of experience. It is the whole working philosophy that includes work ethics, motivation, efforts coupled with applicable experience and a professional way of thinking and problem solving. The ability to anticipate problems and prepare for them in advance is of paramount importance in my occupation. However, some obstacles are very difficult, if not impossible to predict or anticipate. One of our current problems is _____. It hasn't happened before, and I have to come up with strategies that will help us solve it.

## Risk taking

*Risk varies inversely with knowledge.*

Irving Fisher, *The Theory of Interest*

The first two questions under this heading require specific answers, so instead of giving you a complete model answer, I thought it more appropriate to mention a few important points. Use examples that will reinforce your image as a person prepared to take calculated risks when necessary, but also to postpone a decision in certain circumstances in order to gather the information needed to make the right decision.

1   **What was the most risky decision you ever made? What was the outcome of that decision?**

2   **Describe a recent decision you made that involved more than the usual amount of risk.**

3   **Have you made any decisions without having all the necessary information? Why did you make those decisions without waiting for complete information?**

A:   On one occasion I did make a decision without having complete information on the possible solutions. What I did know, however, was the problem, its symptoms and origins, and its potential impact on production and equipment. When I made the decision, prompt and energetic action was needed to prevent a major breakdown. However, although taking a calculated risk can sometimes be justified, playing it safe is usually a much better approach.

4   **Describe a situation in which you received a new procedure or instructions with which you disagreed. What action did you take and why?**

A:   Although that shouldn't be the case, procedures and instructions are sometimes written by non-experts. Whenever I faced such a situation in the past, I made sure I talked to the originator of the particular material and to my superiors, explained why I disagreed and suggested corrections or measures for improving the inadequacies. (*Now add an example from your own experience.*)

5   **Tell me about a time when, after considering all the pros and cons, you decided not to take any action, although you were under pressure to do so.**

*The best reason you could use for postponing action would be waiting for the complete, or at least essential, information, in order to prevent impulsive or irresponsible decision making. That will help you project an image of a systematic, organized and cool-headed achiever, instead of a whimsical guesser.*

6  **Do you think large companies, like your present employer, discourage employees from taking risks?**

*There are two possible paths here. If the company you are being interviewed by is one of the 'heavyweights', your answer is obvious. You like big. Big is beautiful and big can (and does) encourage people to experiment and take risks. If you are interviewing for a position with a smaller company, use this as one of your reasons for leaving or looking for another job with a smaller and more dynamic company, which encourages people to take risks. You like taking calculated risks, can display a successful history of good decisions and thrive on challenge.*

7  **Are there areas in your current job in which you feel you should have a decision-making authority but do not?**

*This question gives you the chance to explore once more your capabilities and resources that haven't been fully utilized or officially recognized by your employer. However, be careful not to sound bitter or disappointed and don't display resentment or frustration with your current employer (which is very easy, because it's probably one of the main reasons you are looking for another job!).*

## Safety

In today's employment climate, clouded with potential threats to employers, such as law suits, damage claims, worker's compensation payments and hefty penalties from various government departments, safety comes first and foremost. Reflect on that in your answers.

1  **Occasionally we have to bend some safety rules to get a particular job done. Have you ever done that and what was the outcome of your decision?**

A:  I always observe safety rules and only in exceptional situations allow myself or my co-workers to 'bend' them a bit to get the job done. A few months ago _____. (*Give an example which involves a safe alternative to standard procedure and stress a satisfactory outcome which saved both time and money.*)

2  **Describe a situation when you noticed some task that was being done unsafely or some process that created a safety hazard. What did you do?**

A:  Quite a few times I have noticed tasks being performed in an unsafe or inefficient manner. On one occasion _____ (*give example*). I wasn't involved in that project, but I warned the workers immediately and corrective action was taken. I also informed their supervisor. At the next safety meeting a new procedure was agreed upon and we haven't had any similar incidents since.

3   **Have you ever had to reprimand or discipline an employee for not observing or violating safety rules?**

A:  I have had to deal with frequent breaches of safety rules and company policies. Most incidents were of a repetitive nature _____ (*people not wearing safety glasses or hearing protection, not using the right tools, improper handling or weight lifting, etc.*). I recognized it as a potential problem and enforced firm rules for breaching them. The number of incidents of that kind has dropped significantly since then, and every employee now recognizes the importance of safety rules.

4   **Have you ever noticed a health or safety hazard before your colleagues or superiors? What was the problem and what course of action did you take?**

A:  On a few occasions I was the first one to recognize a safety hazard. My experience in _____ (*fire fighting, waste management, maintenance methods …*) helped me in discovering potential hazards and taking action to remove those dangers from the workplace. Whenever I notice something irregular or unsafe, I do the initial investigation and inform the internal safety committee.

5   **Have you ever been injured on the job? What happened and what was the outcome of that accident?**

*Complete honesty is needed here. This type of information can be checked from files and records, and if you suffered any permanent damage the fact will be revealed during a medical examination.*

A:  No, I was never injured on the job. Observing safety rules is one of my first priorities, and everything I do, I do in as safe and efficient a manner as possible.

*or*

I suffered a _____ (*name injury*) injury (*ten, five, two …*) years ago. Although I wore the personal safety equipment at the time and observed all safety rules, due to _____ (*failure of machinery, equipment breakdown, low safety standards …*) the injury occurred. I eventually fully recovered and suffer no disability of any kind.

## Awareness (internal/external)

1   Tell me about some departments you interface with in your present position.

    *Explain the relationship and mutual dependency between your department and other departments and the frequency and methods used in communicating with them.*

2   What do you do when unable to solve a problem within your department?

A:  To achieve results in the shortest possible time we have to work closely with other departments. When I face a problem on which we need outside help, I explore all possibilities and consult with my peers from other departments. Sometimes they suggest a specific action and help us perform the actual tasks or provide the complete solution for us. Which way is better or more efficient depends on a particular problem and in-house expertise.

3   What organizational resources or services do you use most often?

    *Depending on your job, you may be using drafting, secretarial, engineering, security services, or any other resources. Contract work force and temporary employees could also be mentioned.*

4   How do you keep informed about new developments in other departments?

A:  The best way to keep informed on new developments is through regular contacts with my colleagues in those departments, either personally or over the phone, and through departmental meetings which are held once a week. They also keep me informed through internal memos and notes.

5   What methods do you use to find out what your competitors are doing?

A:  I use a number of methods. Professional, trade and business magazines and other publications are a vital source of general information. I also cultivate business contacts through my colleagues in those companies. 'Inside' information is very valuable. Trade shows and exhibitions are great places to meet people and talk to them and an opportunity to evaluate products and services. Last, but not least, through regular contact with our suppliers and vendors I usually find out some relevant information on other companies and their plans.

6 **What government bodies affect your company's operations and how?**

*The answer to this question has to be tailored to suit your situation and the business you are in. Since you don't know the interviewer's attitude towards government departments, don't criticize, condemn or complain! Explain the difficulties you face and the steps you take to resolve them. The same applies for the next two questions.*

7 **What future trends do you see in this industry?**

*Make sure you include positive and optimistic statements regarding the company that is interviewing you, even if the future is gloomy. Don't be too pessimistic. Project enthusiasm and strong belief in the future.*

8 **What events outside your company affected your operations in the last year or two? How did you adapt to those changes?**

*This is where your general knowledge of your industry comes in handy. Some of the factors/events/developments you could mention include new government policies and regulations, changes in the market, your competitors' actions, recession, deregulation of the market. The main point is to appear aware of the latest developments and to project a flexible attitude by giving them examples of your positive response to those changes.*

## Career goals

*My interest is in the future because I am going to spend the rest of my life there.*

Charles F. Kettering

1 **What are your career goals for the next five years? How do you plan to achieve them?**

A: My career plan for the next few years is to further improve my management and interpersonal skills and assume higher responsibilities at _____ (*specify your goals*). To achieve that aim I'm planning to continue/start my postgraduate studies in management and find a challenging position with room for personal and professional growth and opportunities for achieving tangible results and professional advancement. This is where this position fits into my career goals. It suits my abilities well and opens new opportunities for achieving success, which is my ultimate goal.

2 **Where do you see yourself in ten years' time?**

*Some interviewers will ask you a question about your long-term goals and plans for achieving them. It's a difficult question to answer, but try to prepare yourself. Don't reply with something smart and ambitious like 'Sitting in your chair'. Nobody likes jokes at their expense.*

A: In the next ten years I expect to progress through _____ (*junior staff, management ...*) to _____ (*management, supervisory, senior management ...*). By that time I will have further improved my technical skills and acquired business-management skills.

3 **What steps have you already taken in order to achieve your goals?**

A: One of the most significant steps I've taken was applying for this job. The position could be significant for my future development, as would be the additional qualifications I'm planning to obtain within _____ years. I have already started my further education in the area of _____ (*computer science, management techniques ...*).

4 **How does your current job relate to your career goals?**

*For people staying in the same career:*

A: My present/former position fits/fitted well in my career plans. I have learned a lot on that job, improved myself and my performance, achieved positive results and advanced through the levels. However, my current opportunities are somewhat limited there, so I think that the time has come to move on. I'm ready for new challenges and increased responsibilities.

*For people changing careers:*

After _____ (*number of years*) in _____ (*present or former occupation*) I've decided to move into _____ (*new profession*). This career turnaround hasn't come suddenly; I have always liked that profession and gradually mastered the skills needed to perform its tasks. I am ready to assume responsibility and start achieving results.

5 **Why do you think this job would help you achieve your career goals?**

*Important question. Prepare your answer carefully so you can show them that you understand the job you've been interviewed for and convince them that it matches your career plans.*

**A:** I see this job as an opportunity to learn more about _____ (*marketing, desktop publishing, management ...*) and to use my skills to the fullest. This experience should assist me with my plans to become a _____ (*solicitor, chief engineer, senior lecturer ...*) within the next three years.

6 **What were your career goals when you graduated/left school? Do you think you have achieved them?**

**A:** After graduation, my main aim was to learn as much as possible in my chosen field. My first job with _____ (*company*) was in line with that plan and helped me develop my potential. Another significant goal was to keep learning and improving my skills, not only on the job but also through formal training and education towards a higher degree. I like my chosen field and I'm satisfied with the progression of my career so far, so I think I have achieved my original goals.

7 **Have you considered any alternative career path for the future?**

**A:** I am very happy with my chosen profession and the progression of my career so far, so I haven't contemplated changing careers. However, should the right opportunity arise, I would consider such a move. I consider myself very flexible and I leave my options open.

8 **Should you be offered this job, when would you expect a promotion?**

**A:** I believe promotions should not be expected, they should be earned. After mastering this position, successfully completing my tasks and making a significant contribution to this company I would be ready for new achievements, should the opportunity arise.

9 **How long would you stay with the company should you get this job?**

**A:** This position fits well into my career plans and I can see a lot of potential for growth in your company. I expect to start being productive very early, and as long as I keep developing my skills, contributing to the company's success and growing on the job, there would be no reason for me to leave.

**10 How important to you is the opportunity to advance your career and, eventually, to reach the top?**

**A:** Reaching the top is a very relative term. Doing a good and professional job is the most important issue to me. Once you concentrate on good performance and on constant improvement of your knowledge and skills, advancement will come naturally. If by reaching the top you mean being a top performer and being successful in my occupation, I do consider reaching the top as very important.

**11 Would you consider switching careers in the future, should the opportunity arise?**

*The answer to this question should be similar to the answer to question 7.*

**12 How long have you been looking for a job?**

*Even if you have been seeking alternative employment for some time, do not admit it. Tell them that you've just started to look for another job. The story is different if you are unemployed. In that case the interviewer probably won't ask you this question. The answer would be obvious from your résumé.*

**A:** This is my first interview for some time. Although I have been monitoring the job market closely, I've decided to seek alternative employment very recently. The downturn in the industry, lack of opportunities at my present position and my readiness for new achievements prompted me to look for other opportunities.

**13 Have you had interviews with other companies recently? How did you get on?**

*This is a typical knockout question. Beware. Never admit that you were unsuccessful at other interviews. The interviewer's logic is: 'If he wasn't good enough for them he can't be good for us, either.'*

**A:** I haven't had any recent interviews, but in the past a very high percentage of my interviews resulted in job offers. The employers recognized my talents and experience and offered me positions of increased responsibilities.

**14 What references do you think your current employer would give you?**

**A:** All my references have always been very good, so I am sure that my present employer would give me an excellent reference.

15 **Does your present employer know that you have been looking for another job?**

A: I haven't told my present employer that I've been exploring other employment possibilities. Once I'm offered a job, I would let them know about my plans and intentions.

*or*

Yes, my employer knows that I have been exploring other employment opportunities, but should you wish to talk to them, please let me know in advance, so I can talk to them first.

# Work experience and employment history

*The way to avoid mistakes is to gain experience. The way to gain experience is to make mistakes.*

Job hunters' Catch 22

1 **How did you get your first job after graduation? How difficult was it to get into _____ (the oil and gas industry, mining, the hospitality industry, corporate finance …)?**

A: During my summer holidays I worked for a few well known companies in my field. I gained valuable experience there and established important business contacts. After graduation one of those companies had a position for a graduate _____ (*surveyor, chemist, engineer* …). The position called for someone with strong interpersonal and analytical skills and a good honours degree. I was selected from the pool of applicants and given a chance to learn and prove myself on that demanding but interesting job.

2 **How do you think you benefited from your first job? What do you consider the most valuable experience gained on that job?**

A: Transition from university to industry was a crucial step in my career. Education prepared me well for the intellectual challenges that lay ahead, but most practical skills I possess I have learned on the job. I have learned how to apply my knowledge to a variety of problems, how to make decisions and set goals and priorities. I became familiar with standards, legal requirements of the profession and various policies and procedures. I would consider the most valuable experiences I gained on that job to be the ability to relate to people and work as part of a team and to achieve tangible results.

3 **Why did you leave your job at _____ company? Did you consider that move to be a promotion or a lateral move?**

A: Although I learned a lot on that job, I felt that while I was specializing in certain areas I lacked experience in other aspects of the job. My subsequent position offered new challenges and opportunities for growth on the job. I gained a much broader range of skills and was given more responsibility. I consider that move, which was by no means a lateral one, the best decision in my career so far.

4 **Have you ever changed jobs or companies purely for monetary gain?**

*Your answer should be **no**. You have to project an image of a person who values the company, the job and your co-workers more than monetary rewards.*

A: Although I consider remuneration as an important motivational factor, the monetary side of a job is of secondary importance. The job itself, its tasks, the work environment and the opportunity to learn and participate in new and exciting developments and become an efficient member of a team are to me the most significant aspects of a job. When I changed jobs, it was never for monetary gain only, but for those factors.

5 **Have your ever been promoted within the same company? How did you feel about that move? Was it in line with your career objectives?**

*If you have been promoted, mention your strengths, qualities and achievements that were the reason for promotion. Emphasize that you welcomed the promotion and were further motivated by additional authority and responsibilities.*

6 **Why were you retrenched from your job with _____ ?**

*It's no shame to be retrenched. If your job was made redundant, it's a company's failure, not yours. Despite giving your best, your employer didn't know how to use your talents and abilities. It's the sad old story – people get blamed for the failure of the system. Employers will never admit that their systems are wrong; it's much easier to blame individuals.*

A: At the time the company was going through a long period of heavy losses, due to bad management and the impact of the recession on the industry. Some radical actions were taken by senior management, and the whole supervisory and some professional levels were made redundant. Sadly, the criteria were not performance and individual efforts, but rather the length of service and the nature of the position. As I was one of the newer employees, my position was terminated.

7  **What areas or aspects of your present/previous job do/did you like most?**

*When answering this question, make sure you address some aspects of the job you have applied for, in order to create the impression that you would like the same things in your new job, should you get it.*

A:  I certainly like some aspects of my present job. It's a dynamic, hard-driving job that requires good decision-making and communication skills. I like constant interaction with people and the benefits of working in a team with other professionals. The job has enabled me to further strengthen my _____ (*practical, theoretical, management ...*) skills and prepared me well for my future career.

8  **Are there any tasks or areas of your present position that have changed since you started on that job?**

*There is no such thing as a static job. Every job changes from time to time and your aim here is to emphasize the positive changes that took place, especially if it was you who initiated them and/or carried them out.*

A:  From the day I started in my present position I kept learning and growing on the job. I have put in a lot of time and effort to my career. As I mastered the job, my tasks became more and more complex and demanding. I became involved in various additional activities and the whole scope of the position changed. I was given more authority and made responsible for _____ . That way I was able to broaden my experience and update my skills and knowledge related to those activities.

9  **I see from your résumé that you owned a small business a couple of years ago. How much benefit did you get out of that experience?**

*Designed for people who owned a small business but, due to various problems, went back to the relative security of permanent employment, this question could invoke bitterness and resignation. Don't let it happen. Emphasize the positive aspects and all the useful things that you learned as a business owner, from accounting to orientation towards customer satisfaction.*

A: The experience I gained while running a small business has proved extremely valuable. I acquired a good working knowledge of various disciplines such as accounting, taxation, profit and loss control, logistics, negotiation and planning. I learned even more about people, how to treat customers and vendors, how to obtain their co-operation and how to keep them happy and satisfied with my products and services.

10 **Tell me about some of the knowledge and experience you have gained in your present position that you could use in this job.**

*Always keep in mind that employers try to predict your future behaviour and achievements on the basis of your past. They reason that everything you've done in the past will be, or at least could be, repeated in future. That applies to both your strong points and achievements and to your shortcomings and mistakes. This question confirms that line of thinking. To answer it, you have to know the job you've applied for really well, and use that knowledge when emphasizing your capabilities in performing the main tasks of the position.*

11 **What are the reasons for the gaps in your employment history?**

*This answer will again depend on your particular situation. The interviewer wants you to relate the reasons for those gaps – maternity leave, serious or prolonged illness or disability, inability to find any work, periods spent at home taking care of your family, etc. Whatever your reasons, always emphasize the fact that you were able to re-enter the work force and achieve results in new jobs. Your explanation of the facts should be concise and to the point. Don't beat about the bush, avoid answering or blame others. Flawless careers are rare, we are all human and we all make mistakes.*

12 **You have changed jobs quite a few times within the last few years. What were the reasons for that?**

*Even if it's true, don't say something like 'I usually get bored doing the same job after a couple of years, so I look for a change' or 'I had some debts, so I used every opportunity to get a better paying job'.*

A: I've changed jobs according to my career plans. The main reason was to gain experience in various aspects of

_____ (*management, medicine, human resource management* ...) and broaden my horizons. I was able to recognize opportunities and capitalize on them.

13 **Would you recommend your present employer to others?**

*Another knockout question. Say only good things about your former or current employer. Your message should be: 'It's a great place to work' (but not for you).*

A: I can say only good things about my present employer. I was treated with respect and given every opportunity to participate in various activities and achieve both the employer's and my own goals. Due to the _____ (*downturn in the industry, lack of funds or new contracts, company's restructuring plans, limited opportunities for advancement* ...) I have decided to explore other employment opportunities. However, for someone with less experience who is interested in that type of work, it would be a great place to work.

14 **What do you consider your biggest achievement or the most important idea you have implemented in your career?**

*The answer has to be tailored to suit your work experience. Although the question asks for the single most important contribution, you can mention more than one, especially if they could be relevant to the company that's interviewing you.*

15 **I've heard stories about the bad feelings between your present employer and unions and how badly the company treats its employees. Are they true?**

*Another knockout question. Never discuss rumours about your employer, or (heaven forbid!) internal secrets and confidential information. You have to project an image of a trustworthy employee who can keep secrets and be loyal to his employer. If you badmouth your present employer, the interviewers can expect the same to happen to them further down the track.*

A: I'm really not sure. I haven't heard any such rumours myself. My priority is to concentrate on my performance and represent the company to the best of my abilities. To me, there is no room for rumours in a productive environment, where lines of communication are open.

# Suitability for the job

**1  Why would you like to work for this company?**

*This is probably the most important question in every job interview. You can be sure that this question will be on every interviewer's list and you should prepare yourself for it. Spend as much time as you need preparing your answer; your efforts will be rewarded. The next question is similar and should be treated with equal respect.*

**2  Why did you apply for this particular position?**

**A:** First and foremost, I'm well qualified for this job and able to make a significant contribution to your company. This position suits my skills, talents and career plans, and has a lot of advancement opportunities. Last, but not least, the outstanding reputation of your company was a significant factor that influenced my decision to apply for this position.

**3  How will our company benefit from hiring you?**

*This question is a natural follow-on from the previous ones. Even if they don't ask you this question directly, it is always on their mind, and whatever you say at a job interview should address this question in one way or another. This is a very important opportunity to summarize all your strong points, skills and abilities and to talk in terms of benefits. Put yourself in the employer's shoes and tell them everything you can do for them.*

**4  What do you know about our company?**

*This is a good opportunity to display your knowledge and show them that you've thoroughly researched the company. Start with the company's mission statement, main locations, products, key people. Cover the current plans and actions, such as expansions, investments, and finish with future plans, long-range goals and your view of the company's future (remember to make it a rosy one). Always project enthusiasm and sincere interest. Don't criticize, condemn or complain.*

**5  Do you have any friends or relatives working for this company?**

If you do, say so. That fact can be checked, so truth is best here. In some cases, having a relative who is a hard worker and a reputable person may help you to also be perceived thus.

**A:** A good friend of mine works in your _____ office. I don't know anybody here in _____.

6  **How did you find out about this vacancy?**

*If the vacancy was advertised, you probably won't be asked this question. If it wasn't, tell them the truth: a friend told you about it, you offered your services without knowing that there was a vacancy, or whatever the case is.*

A:  I have been interested in your company for some time, so I was familiar with your plans for expansion and growth and anticipated a vacancy of this kind. I then decided to offer my services to you.

7  **How confident are you in your ability to handle this position?**

A:  I am very confident in my abilities. I learn quickly and it shouldn't take me long to achieve results in this job. Every beginning is difficult, but I always make an extra effort to become productive in the shortest time possible. I already know most of the job requirements, so once I have familiarized myself with the place and established the right relationships with other members of the team, all the ingredients for success will be there.

8  **What particular strengths and qualifications would you bring to this job?**

*Similar to the previous question, just shift the emphasis from their benefits to your capabilities and strengths.*

9  **Do you think your lack of experience could affect your performance on this job?**

*You'll have to compensate for any lack of experience. Use experience gained in similar areas, portable skills (the ones you can apply on the new job) and your knowledge as substitutes for relevant experience.*

A:  I may not have many years of experience in this field, but my knowledge and ability to learn quickly and work hard will enable me to make immediate contributions and perform on the job. With some specialized training and my desire to learn and improve myself, I could accomplish a lot in this position.

10  **Don't you think you are over-qualified for this position?**

*They fear that you will leave as soon as a better opportunity comes up. You have to reassure them using the following ideas: there are always new things to be learned in any job, you are particularly interested in that job and you would stay as long as you keep growing on the job and contributing to the employer's success. This question can also be a hint that you are too old for a job or that they can't pay you as much money as you were earning before.*

**A:** In every position there are always new skills to be mastered and new knowledge to be acquired. However, my experience in similar positions would enable me to do the required tasks fast, with confidence and with minimum training and supervision. The company would not have to train me in all aspects of the job, so there would be an immediate return on your investment in me and my services. This company provides a lot of opportunities for people with talent and the right qualifications, and could certainly benefit from my knowledge.

**11 Would you agree to a three-month probationary period?**

*Three or six months' probation is mandatory with some employers (especially government departments); it's got nothing to do with your abilities. If that's not the case, the interviewer is not totally convinced that you are the ideal person for the job, so you have to reassure him.*

**A:** I can see no problems with a probationary period. I am a fast learner and it shouldn't take me long to prove myself and assume all the responsibilities of the position.

**12 Are you prepared to accept a position as a trainee?**

*If you are, say so. If not, tell them why. Some employers cannot comprehend that a person of talent and experience would be insulted to start at the bottom. If you start low, it's going to take a long while to reach the top. Some employers will try to get you cheap by asking you to start at the entry level. Their usual justification is lack of relevant experience. Don't fall for this trick.*

**A:** Yes, I am. I haven't had much experience in this area and I would welcome the opportunity to learn on this job and get a good foundation in this business. I can use a good deal of my knowledge and experience, so it shouldn't take me long to master this job and assume bigger responsibilities.

*or*

I have had a number of years of related experience, so all I need to learn are some specific details and methods this company uses, which should not take long. I am capable of doing all the tasks required by this position efficiently and without supervision. I'm a self-starter and can bring maturity and responsibility to this position. You could use my strengths and talents much better in a higher and more demanding position.

13  **Do you think you possess a skill or knowledge that could give you an edge over other candidates?**

*A ridiculous question but, sadly, a very common one. How would you know who your competitors are? The best strategy is to tell them you are not familiar with your competitors' skills and knowledge, and then repeat again what your strengths are and what you could do for the employer if selected.*

14  **Are you looking for a permanent or temporary assignment?**

*By the time you reach an interview, it should be clear both to you and to the interviewer what type of position you have applied for, so this question will not be asked too often. Should you approach an employer directly, without an advertised vacancy, you can expect this question.*

A:  I have been looking for a permanent position, but should you have a temporary opening only, I may be prepared to accept it if it fits into my career plans.

15  **This job requires frequent travel. Would that create a problem for you?**

*Count your blessings. You may disagree, but this is your opportunity to travel for free, see places and meet people.*

A:  I have always enjoyed travel. That was one of my reasons for choosing this type of work. I have travelled extensively in the past due to the nature of my positions and I would welcome the opportunity to establish contacts and work in different parts of the country.

16  **Do you have any questions about the company or the vacancy?**

*This is usually the interviewer's last, closing, question. The ball is now in your court, so make sure you kick it hard. This is probably your only opportunity to find out all the fine details about the job and people you'll be working with should you get it.*

*Some typical questions are listed on pages 181–2, but you can ask anything you like. Just make sure that by asking each particular question you gain points. If you are not sure about any question, if there is a danger that the question may make you look ignorant, misinformed, naive, boasting, selfish or insensitive, don't ask it.*

**17 Tell me about some of the first things you would do on this job.**

A: My first task would be to establish a productive and professional relationship with my co-workers. Learning about the company's policies and procedures is another very important step in the familiarization process, as is becoming familiar with all aspects of the position and all job requirements. These initial tasks would make me ready to meet all demands and produce results. I feel very confident in my ability to handle all the tasks required by this job and I would produce results in a very short time.

**18 This is the organization chart for our department. Do you think you could work within this structure?**

A: This organizational structure seems fine to me, and I'm sure I would fit in nicely. The management structure is pretty lean and probably very efficient. The overall scheme looks effective and well balanced.

**19 There are quite a few smokers in our office. As a non-smoker, do you see that as a problem?**

A: As long as my work area is free from smoke I don't mind other people smoking in the building. It's their personal choice. However, if it affected my work and productivity I would classify it as a concern.

**20 Have you got any concerns about this position or the company?**

*This is a good opportunity to ask any questions you want to ask. Don't enquire about money and benefits. Leave that issue for the interviewer to bring up. Concentrate on the position, previous people doing that job, advancement opportunities, training and learning. You can also ask about the company's plans and goals.*

*If you haven't got any questions:*

A: I had many questions, but during our conversation you covered all of them very thoroughly. I now have a detailed picture of the position and the company, and feel that this position suits my skills and talents extremely well.

**21 As a (lawyer, medical practitioner, chartered accountant ...) are you licensed to practise in this country/part of the country?**

*Some professionals need a licence to practice in each country or state they work in. If you've got such a licence, it's a plus. If you haven't, tell them you'll get it as soon as possible.*

**22** Do you have your own tools and equipment necessary for the job?

**A:** I have made an investment in the equipment needed to do my job properly and professionally. (*List some examples, and don't forget your professional library, if relevant.*)
*or*
The equipment and tools I needed on the job were provided by my employer. However, if this position requires them, I would be happy to buy my own.

**23** Should you be offered this position, when could you start?

**A:** I have to give my present employer _____ (*give period*) notice. If it suits you, I could start right after that period. I would prefer an early start myself, so I can meet my future colleagues and prove myself on the job as soon as possible.

# Outside interests

*What we do during our working hours determines what we have; what we do in our leisure hours determines what we are.*

George Eastman, founder of Kodak

**1** What are your hobbies, interests and leisure time activities?

*This question needs a balanced answer. A bit of this and a bit of that. Betting on two horses is safer than placing all your money on one. If the interviewer looks like a sports-oriented person emphasize your outdoor lifestyle and sports achievements. Passive hobbies (reading, listening to music, chess) are viewed less favourably than active ones by most interviewers. For some 'intellectual' positions, such as educational appointments, research or scientific jobs, physically passive hobbies and interests such as reading, astronomy and writing may be regarded as desirable and project the right image.*

**2** Do you prefer to watch sports events on TV or actively participate in them?

*Active participation in sports is viewed favourably. It tells the interviewer that you are a team player and that you know how to observe the rules and work towards a common goal. Watching sports events on TV makes you a couch potato.*

**A:** Although I don't mind watching top sporting events occasionally, I prefer active participation, especially in team sports. It helps me keep fit and feel good, and is a great way of meeting people and socializing.

3 **Do you prefer team sports or individual ones?**

*If the job you applied for requires team work (most jobs do), tell them you prefer team sports. If it's a 'lone wolf job' (astronomer, writer …) individuality is a plus.*

**A:** I don't differentiate between team and individual sports. Both kinds have their strong points: teamwork and team spirit on one side and individual strength and self-reliance on the other. To me, the most important aspects of sport are achievement and hard work. I prefer active participation in sports. Apart from the obvious benefits, such as fitness and stamina, sport helps me develop my people-management skills, team spirit and ability to work with others towards a common goal.

4 **What is your favourite sport?**

*The answer should be similar to the one in the previous question. Don't mention any destructive sport, such as boxing or mud-wrestling, unless applying for a position where those skills could prove useful (a bouncer in a night club, police officer or bodyguard).*

5 **What newspapers and magazines do you read regularly?**

The safest bet is to go for trade or professional magazines. Tell them you read *Penthouse* or *OK!* and watch the lights go out.

**A:** I regularly read professional magazines such as _____, to which I have a subscription. My partner is subscribed to _____, which I also find very informative.

6 **Do you have a subscription to any of them?**

**A:** I am subscribed to _____. This magazine covers a wide range of business and management topics as well as current trends and news.

7 **What sections in a newspaper or a magazine do you find most interesting?**

*It would be a mistake to offer the sports pages or comics as an answer (although I know many professional people – I didn't say 'highly educated' – who read only the sports pages). The business section is always the safest bet,* although anything that can help you project a systematic, business-oriented and creative image is welcome. Current affairs (local, national and international) is also a safe bet, but use it as a last resort.

**8   What are your favourite TV programmes?**

*This is a knockout question. Avoid brain-washers like soap operas or light sit-com. Go for something scientific, businesslike or political.*

**A:** I don't have much time for television. It's not high on my list of priorities, but I enjoy some programmes, such as news, current affairs, business reviews and scientific programmes.

**9   Does your social life include colleagues or co-workers?**

*Tell them you don't differentiate between people. Your friends come from all spheres of life. Some of them are old school friends, some are colleagues or business acquaintances. That projects a balanced attitude towards life and relationships.*

**A:** Some of my friends are also my co-workers. We share interests and lifestyle and feel close to each other, probably due to our close and productive relationships at work. I have many other friends and acquaintances, old friends from school and university, neighbours and others.

**10  Do you prefer activities at home, with your family, or an outdoor lifestyle?**

*A balanced approached is needed again. Since you work hard and long hours, you don't have much leisure time. For that reason you use every minute of it to be with your family, either indoors or outdoors.*

**A:** I try to mix both, if possible. During the summer, we tend to spend most our time together outside the house, around the pool, in the country or playing sports. In winter, because the weather conditions are less favourable, much more time is spent indoors or visiting friends.

**11  What types of books do you like? Can you name a few of your favourites?**

*Don't mention this book or any other book on interviewing or job hunting. Don't even mention self-improvement books. Select something appropriate – not too shallow or scandalous, not too intellectual. Moderation is needed here. Autobiographies of successful business people are not a bad choice.*

**12  Do you drink alcohol at home or in social occasions?**
*Never admit that you drink more than normal amounts.
The occasional glass of wine or a beer with friends is OK.
And another point – never drink before an interview. Some
people go for a nip of spirit 'for courage'. Don't. Use coffee
or herbal teas for their calming effect (if you are a nervous
type). Never concede that you drink alone. It creates a bad
image of antisocial behaviour; most alcoholics drink alone.*
**A:**  I don't mind an occasional drink with friends or business
partners, but drinking is not really my game.

## Salary history and requirements

All the questions in this section serve the same purpose. They
help the employer to establish your price – the lowest offer you
would accept. The starting salary is extremely important, due to
the fact that employers think in percentage points. They say:
'Last year we gave you a ten per cent rise while the management
got only five!', forgetting that 10 per cent of say, £25,000 is
much less than 5 per cent of £75,000! If you start low, it's very
difficult to get a decent rise (in absolute terms).

Your salary history should be used only as an indication of your
progress and achievements. Past salary levels should have
nothing to do with your future salary. Each job is different and
the remuneration packages have to be different. By telling the
interviewers your present or previous salary, you automatically
place an upper limit on their offer.

If you have to tell them the figure, think of all possible benefits
you are or were getting and add 5 to 10 per cent to it. Find out
how much a company car, say, is worth to your present
employer. It may be worth only £4,000 per year to you, but it's
probably worth close to £7,000 or £10,000 to them. In short –
boost it. Even if they try to check your salary, your former
employers will not tell them. The secrecy of the pay-system is
finally working for you!

**1  Can you give me a short overview of your salary history?**
*Avoid numbers, if you can. Concentrate on other benefits
such as job satisfaction, personal growth and improvement
or increased achievements.*
**A:**  I would be glad to tell you exact figures and dates, but I am
not able to recite them from memory, due to regular pay
increases and promotions. The money side of those jobs was

not as important to me as the opportunity to learn and perform on the job. My employment record shows a continuous trend in salary growth.

**2  Have you ever been refused a salary increase (pay rise)?**

**A:** Due to my positive performance appraisals I haven't had to ask for a pay rise. The salary reviews resulted in consistent increases in line with my contributions. That means I was never refused a raise on the basis of inadequate performance.

**3  What is your present salary?**

*Make sure you take every penny into account. The higher you can come up without lying, the stronger your bargaining position will be. Start low and they'll offer you peanuts. We all know what happens to employers who pay peanuts – they get monkeys!*

**A:** With bonus, overtime, company contributions to my superannuation fund, leave loading and a company car my package is around £54,000 per year.

**4  How much would you like to be earning in 5 or 10 years time?**

**A:** I constantly strive to achieve above average results and to contribute to my company's profitability, so I expect the remuneration to reflect my efforts and contributions to my employer and to be competitive with what similar positions pay of that time.

**5  What salary do you think you are worth?**

**A:** Our worth is measured by our contributions to our employer. My personal credo is to perform to the best of my abilities and to contribute as much as I can. Therefore, I expect to advance in accordance with my efforts and achieved results and I'm sure that the right employer will recognize a job well done and be fair in putting a value tag on my work.

**6  Do you think people in your occupation are paid enough?**

*Be careful. You are treading on thin ice. Some people are grossly underpaid. If you are one of them, keep it to yourself. Don't let your anger and frustration show! There is nothing you can gain by speaking up (it is very unlikely that they would change their salary structure just because of you), but there is a lot to lose.*

**A:** I think that no matter how much people earn, they would always strive for more. It seems that's human nature. However, the answer to this question is a very complex one. There are quite a few factors to be considered, such as the status of a particular profession in society, education levels, supply and demand for that type of services, contribution to the community as a whole, and, above all, the competence and integrity of the person doing the job. The most important aspect is the contribution people make to their employers and the quality of their work. The rewards usually follow automatically.

7 **Should you join this company, would you be interested in becoming a member of our pension plan?**
*Your message should reflect your attitude: you are not thinking about retirement, only about contributing to the well-being of the company that is interviewing you.*

**A:** After a careful consideration of the plan's structure and competitiveness in the financial market, I would be happy to join the plan should it prove to be performing and providing a good return on the invested funds.

8 **Do you have any additional income?**
*This is none of their business. If you want to be honest, go ahead, but you may risk being offered a lower salary. Remember the employers' tendency to pay peanuts and expect a miraculous performer on their payroll? This question is one of their tools for saving some money. I prefer the second option – no outside income.*

**A:** I occasionally do some _____ (*baby sitting, tutoring ...*) in the evenings and some part-time work on weekends as a (*bartender, gardener, handyman ...*) but I have no regular commitments that could have an impact on my job. It is purely an extra source of income to help me achieve my financial goals.
*or*
I don't have any outside income (*a much better answer*).

9 **How much would you lower your expectations if the salary you are aiming for is higher than the salary package we are offering for this position?**
*This smart question demands a smart answer. The core of it is: I am not prepared to lower my expectations. Wrap it up and you get this:*

**A:** The salary itself is just one component of the whole offer. Should the working conditions, future prospects and opportunities for advancement be favourable, I would consider a figure slightly below my expectations. However, it would be difficult to accept less than my present salary. My salary history shows a consistent upward trend, as a direct consequence of my performance and achievements, and I intend to continue that trend.

**10  To be honest, we'll have to decide between you and another candidate. We think either of you would be suitable for the job, so it comes down to money. What is the lowest salary you are prepared to accept?**

*Beware of this question. Whoever uses this tactic must be a shrewd interviewer, intimidating you and playing you against other candidates. You can bet that the other candidates were asked the same question.*

**A:** My work record shows increasing levels of responsibility and achievement and my salary history follows that trend. For a person with my qualifications and experience, and taking into account the complexity and the importance of this position and the contributions that I could make on this job, a salary of _____ (*name the lowest figure you would accept*) is an absolute minimum.

# Your questions for the interviewer

*It is better to know some of the questions than to know all of the answers.*

James Thurber

## About the company/department

- What are the company's plans for the future?
- What new products is the company working on and planning to introduce?
- How does the company compare with its competitors?
- Is the company considering opening new plants or new ventures and acquisitions?
- Are any cuts in the work force planned for the immediate future?
- How is the department organized?

- How is the department viewed by the management and other departments?
- What are the department's overall functions and responsibilities?

## About the position

- How long has the position been vacant?
- How many employees have held the position in the last five/ten years?
- Why have they left?
- What are the most important duties of the position as perceived by the company?
- How much have the position, its duties and scope changed in the last five/ten years?
- How does the position fit into the overall company structure?

## About your direct supervisor

- Who does the position report to?
- Who does the supervisor report to?
- What is the supervisor's background?
- What is the supervisor's management style?

## About salary and benefits

- Does the company have a formal salary structure with well defined levels or a more flexible one?
- What is the salary range for this position?
- How often are salaries reviewed?
- What factors determine the reviewed salary levels?
- Are there any incentive schemes in place?
- What insurance benefits are provided by the company?
- Is there a profit-sharing scheme?
- Are relocation expenses met by the company?
- Is there a superannuation plan available? How much does the company contribute? How much do the employees contribute?
- Is there any annual leave loading?

## About advancement opportunities

- How many employees have been promoted from the position in the last five/ten years?
- What are the opportunities for advancement into management?
- Are there formal training programmes available? How do they work?
- What factors are used to determine promotion eligibility?

# Illegal questions

Twenty years ago, employers had few legal obligations in the hiring process. Today, things are very different. A myriad of laws, legislation and acts affects the process. Interviewers are very limited in the questions they are allowed to ask. The following information should not be used in the hiring process and any question addressing these issues may be illegal:

- race
- religion
- national origin
- marital status
- sex (gender)
- number of children
- affiliations and membership of legal organizations
- handicaps.

Any question that deals with the issues listed above may breach one or more laws and acts. Your task is to recognize those questions and form your answers in one of the few possible ways. Of course, not every question probing those areas is illegal – what can make it illegal is the way the each particular question is asked! Basically, anything that bears no significance to the job you have applied for or to your capability to perform on that job is irrelevant and probably illegal! When asked an illegal question, you have four choices.

## 1: Answer it honestly

This is the best option in some cases, but should the question be intimidating or too personal I would suggest one of the more advanced strategies. If they ask you awkward questions now, can you imagine what working for those people would be like?

### 2: Answer it, but tell them what they want to hear

This is the option I would recommend in most cases. If the interviewer asks you an illegal or tasteless question, you have a moral right not to tell the truth. Illegal questions are always transparent – it's very easy to see what the interviewer is getting at – and therefore it is very easy to fabricate the answer he or she wants to hear.

### 3: Counter-attack with a question, preferably a humorous one

If asked 'What is your religion?' you could say 'Does your firm represent any particular sect?' Or for 'Which method of contraception do you use?', a good answer would be 'Which one do most of your employees prefer?'

### 4: Politely refuse to answer

In an ideal world this would be the ideal response. In the real world, I would not recommend it. In my opinion, by refusing to answer you minimize your chances of getting the job. You may preserve your pride and dignity, but your stomach needs food, remember?

In my view, the best strategy is to try to establish why that particular question was asked. The interviewer may be concerned about a particular aspect or a requirement of the job or about something from your résumé. Instead of directly answering the question asked, you may address the hidden concern instead. One of the reasons interviewers ask questions like 'When do you plan to get married?' or 'How many children do you plan to have?' is that they are concerned you may leave the firm as soon as such an event happens or that you may ask for unpaid leave and they would have to look for a replacement. This type of question is aimed primarily at women, due to employers' perception that most women would put their careers on hold and stay at home with young children while most men would not.

A typical answer addressing such a concern would be 'I know this job involves a significant amount of travel and I can assure you that my family responsibilities will not interfere with my performance on the job.'

# Thinking on your feet

The job interview is an occasion when you may be asked all sorts of questions. Despite what I said earlier (that job interviews are predictable, so you can practise answering questions and prepare yourself for the occasion) it is impossible to prepare tailor-made answers for every possible question.

The ability that will be the most precious in a job interview is the ability to think on your feet, to improvise, to be innovative and creative with your answers. The real art of true guerrilla fighters is to project sincerity, enthusiasm and charisma even when you are inventing material, telling them what they want to hear or grossly generalizing or exaggerating.

The following list contains a few selected topics you could be asked about in various interviewing situations. Try not to write exact answers to each one, just 'frame' your answers and think in terms of what points you would cover and in what order for each subject.

## Some company-related topics

1  What does my company do?
2  My company's main products and strengths.
3  I was on a business trip when ...
4  Why did I choose my present company?
5  What is the best job in my company, and why?
6  My company's main competitors are ...
7  My company's main weaknesses are ...
8  My company's main strengths are ...
9  My company's plans for the future.
10  If I could change something in my company, I would change ...

## General topics

1  I was in a foreign country ...
2  Why did I choose my occupation?
3  A birthday party I enjoyed the most.
4  What do I do to keep fit?
5  The best book I ever read.
6  My most memorable vacation.

7   When I prayed the hardest, and why?
8   My favourite pet.
9   The biggest disappointment in my life.
10   An instance when I regretted saying something.
11   The best advice I have ever received.
12   The best friend I ever had.
13   Something I made myself.
14   The greatest compliment I received.
15   My secret ambition.
16   Things I liked in school.
17   Things I didn't like in school.
18   My favourite newspapers or magazines.
19   What do I think about computers?
20   How I got my first job.
21   Things I don't like on my present job.
22   Things I enjoy in my job.
23   The best investment in my life.
24   The worst investment in my life.
25   Working with people or working with things?
26   A crisis that I or my family faced.
27   The worst travelling experience.
28   My worst day at work.
29   I made an enemy.
30   My friend helped me a lot.
31   What do I like about my home town?
32   The town and country I would like to live in.
33   When I was proud of someone.
34   I offended someone by …
35   Do I believe in horoscopes and why (or why not)?
36   My favourite recipe or dish.
37   When persistence and hard work paid off.
38   My favourite TV show.
39   What I think of the education I got at school or university.
40   Some good and bad aspects of training courses and management seminars.

# The last impression is a lasting impression

*The game isn't over till it's over.*

Yogi Berra

Exit skills are often forgotten assets. Most of us don't like being interviewed and can hardly wait to leave the room once the interview draws to a close. Believe me, the interviewers can sense such keenness. Learn how to exit gracefully so you leave an impression that you enjoyed yourself and would like to stay longer if only they were not so busy. Call it flattery or pretending if you like, but you have obviously noticed that this book is not just about job interviews – it is about *impression management*!

So, before you go for that important job interview, think about what you are going to say first and last. The attention you'll get from the interviewers will peak during the first minute or two and the last moments of your interview. Your last words must help your case and leave a definitive positive impact on the other side. There is only one sure way to achieve this: once you say what you wanted to say, shut up and say no more. Resist the feeling of insecurity which may push you into spouting further drivel. The impact you created will be lessened and the favourable impression lost forever.

The last words you utter before leaving the interview room will make the final impression on the people evaluating you. End it all with a strong note of optimism and confidence.

One always useful finishing exiting tactic is to ask a question. It puts the ball in their court, lifts the pressure from your shoulders and channels the interviewer's efforts towards answering the question, or at least thinking about it, instead of diligently assessing you.

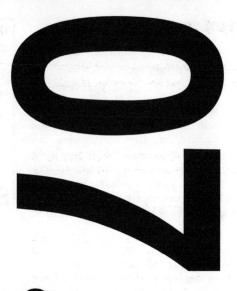

**07**

# closing the deal

In this chapter you will learn:
- some salary negotiating tactics
- how to provide references
- about contracts of employment

# Salary negotiating tactics

*It is a well known proposition that you know who's going to win a negotiation: it's he who pauses the longest.*
Robert Holmes à Court, *Sydney Morning Herald*,
24 May 1986

## Your objectives

In any negotiating process, be it negotiating when buying a house or talking about your future salary, there are two major objectives:

- to change the interviewer's impression of the strength of your position;
- to change the interviewer's impression of the strength of his position.

That's why you should project an image of a job-chooser, not a job-beggar. The interviewer can sense how you feel about yourself. Your task is to lure him into thinking that you have more than one ace up your sleeve. Once he starts thinking that way, your value can go only one way – up.

When the time comes for financial negotiation, what counts is not how much you are really worth, it's how much the interviewer thinks you're worth! Remember these words. At the job interview, which lasts on average an hour or so, you cannot present your *complete self* to the interviewer. All you can create is a positive *image* of yourself, which will make employers eager to have you on their payroll.

Salary negotiation is an elaborate game in which anything can be used as a tool. Bluffing is particularly useful. Employers use it quite often. Whenever they tell you something like: 'The salary for this position is £32,000', or 'We cannot go above £34,000', you know that they are prepared to go as high as £38,000 or even £40,000.

## Money, benefits and substitutes

*A negotiator should observe everything. You must be part Sherlock Holmes, part Sigmund Freud.*
Victor Kiam, *Going For It*

Beware of the substitutes for money. They are usually called benefits. Your main task is to analyse them and to put a price tag on them, to establish how much each benefit is worth to you. Some benefits do have a certain value. They are:

- superannuation (pension plan benefits)
- company cars
- private health insurance
- air fares (for people living and/or working outside major centres)
- leisure days off
- holiday loadings
- bonus schemes
- company share plans (discounted shares)
- subsidized housing
- approved study leave
- subsidized rent, telephone bills, rates, etc.

However, there are some substitutes used by employers to attract the naive candidates. Most of the commonly used substitutes are basically useless from a material point of view.

- **Fancy titles** are a form of psychological compensation. They usually hide dull jobs and make people feel better about themselves doing jobs below their capabilities. How would you like telling your 'potential' girlfriend that you work as a garbage collector or a liftboy? Environmental technician and elevator supervisor sound much nicer.
- **Promises**. Not worth a penny. Once the employer gets you on their payroll, they tend to forget what they promised. Always get promises in writing. Even then, what can you do if the employers don't fulfil them? Complain, threaten legal action and possibly risk being sacked? Not likely.
- **'The opportunity for growth'**. A very common promise in job advertisements. It still isn't clear to me what employers mean by that. Growth of your salary, professional growth, growth of your frustration, or what? In most cases it may mean growth of your responsibilities and increase in overtime work with no reward whatsoever.

## What will your hourly rate be?

One of the shrewdest tactics used by employers is definitely a 'work now, we'll pay you later' philosophy. Any employee who doesn't get paid for overtime is a victim of this plot. They were told that occasional overtime is required and that their salary packages were created with that in mind.

Let me illustrate that with an example. Say you were offered a position as a mechanical engineer, with salary package of $52,000 per annum, which is the current market rate for an engineer with five to seven years of experience. For a standard 40-hour week your hourly rate would be $25. Sounds fine. In a few months' time you realize that, due to the workload, you are actually putting in 55 hours a week. Your effective hourly rate is just over $18 per hour! By accepting these terms you reduced your salary to around $38,000 per annum, which is a starting salary for an inexperienced graduate. So, what have you achieved? You've just gone back five to seven years!

*Never think in 'per annum' terms. What matters is your hourly rate. That's how much you're worth.*

## Superannuation (pension plans)

Most employers offer their employees some sort of a pension plan. Some of them are contributory (employees contribute a certain percentage of their salaries), some aren't. In any case, all they offer is time: the longer you contribute to the fund, the better off you'll be at the end. The basic idea of creating a 'nest-egg' for your retirement is appealing; however, there is another point of view.

Superannuation funds usually reflect the employer's financial position. The better the company's performance, the stronger the fund. There is only one problem: if the company made a profit this year, why do you have to wait 10 or 20 years to get your share? This is a typical 'work now, we'll pay you later' plot. Furthermore, they'll use your money for 10 or 20 years so, basically, you are lending them your money – and, incidentally, being taxed twice in the process (once before they deduct your contributions from your salary, and once when you retire or resign and take the lump sum).

It seems that the whole scheme was designed to ensure the employer's hold over you and take away your freedom of choice. Ambitious people, who want fast advancement, are the ones most affected. No matter when you leave the company, you can be sure that the benefits will be much less than the ones you would receive had you stayed there till retirement.

Avoid companies that use 'Work now, we'll pay you later' tactics.

# References

After the interview, should you be the most promising candidate, the employer will check your references. By that time they are almost certain that you are the person for the job and a reference check is the last obstacle to your new position.

## Written references

Most people ask for a written reference before they leave the company. Some references are purely stating the period of employment, job title and, sometimes, basic duties. They don't address performance, quality of work, personality, strong and weak points or anything similar. That type of reference can serve purely as documentary evidence that you were employed, who your employer was and how long you stayed there. Potential employers are not very interested in that type of reference.

A written reference that provides an employer's view of former employee's skills, performance and achievements is much more useful to your new (still potential) employer. However, there are some differences. A reference typed on personal stationary gets less credence from employers than one on the letterhead of a firm. The employer's view is that in the latter case the opinion is not purely the writer's, but reflects the views of the whole firm. The referee puts his company's credibility behind his opinion.

Some companies don't allow references to be typed on company letterheads. In that case, you can either ask your former boss to add a remark to a reference, explaining that fact, or you can explain it yourself to prospective employers.

There is only one flaw in the whole business with written references, the flaw that seriously undermines their value: the prospective employer knows that every written reference will be a favourable one. I haven't heard of a boss that would write a bad reference and then hand it to the departing employee. The worst that can happen is that your boss may refuse to write you a reference.

## Telephone references

Telephone reference checks are regarded by employers as more revealing. When they talk to your former bosses they look for reluctance or hesitancy on the referee's part. It is much more difficult to praise people in person than in a written form.

The name of the referee will always be given to a prospective employer by a candidate. By choosing a loyal referee candidates try to increase their chances of passing the reference checks. But, quite often, employers want to talk to some other person who knows the candidate as well, not only to the nominated referee. By using this trick, employers get a 'second opinion', which is usually less favourable, due to the fact that the second referee wasn't selected by the candidate.

## Interviewer's tactics

When your interviewer or a person that has to check your references speaks to your former employer, some of the following 'hard' questions will be used (if they do their job properly):

- Would you employ him or her again without hesitation?
- The job we are recruiting for is very challenging. It needs a person with strong skills. Do you really think this person has what it takes?
- What was the candidate's reason for leaving your company?
- What did the candidate achieve while working for you? Did he or she meet the criteria for the job?
- What plans did you have for the candidate? Had they stayed with your company, would you have promoted them or terminated their employment?

In a nutshell, the interviewer will tend to probe as deeply as possible into your relationship with your former employers and gather as much information on your past performance as possible.

## How to get a good reference

Don't burn your bridges. Always part on friendly terms. Write a polite resignation letter and praise your former employer for the encouragement you were given, the opportunities you had and all the nice things they did for you.

When you leave, keep cultivating relationships with your former employers. You will need them to get your next job, and the next one, and the next one … If possible, visit them from time to time, displaying interest in them. Send Christmas cards and regularly keep in touch over the phone.

Also, don't rely on just one referee. If he or she leaves the company, the prospective employer will certainly talk to someone else who is still there, and this person might not like you, know you, or who knows what. Cultivate a 'substitute referee' who can help you with a good reference.

*Remember that by burning your bridges behind you, you may also burn the ones that lie ahead!*

# Paperwork

*A verbal contract isn't worth the paper it's written on.*
Samuel Goldwyn, attributed

## Employment contracts

What is a contract of employment? It is an agreement between an employer and an employee that stipulates every part of the employment relationship, either explicitly or implicitly. The strange aspect of the whole situation is that even if you don't sign a piece of paper with the title 'Contract of Employment', a contract nevertheless exists.

That means that an employment contract can be written, oral or implied! This is the beauty of so called 'Common Law'. Whichever way you look at it, beware (*caveat emptor*)!

To the company a contract says, 'We've got him locked in, so we don't have to worry about him or listen to him as much as if we didn't.' To the individual it says, 'Here is a date when your loyalty expires. Start thinking well in advance about the terms you'll renew.'

*Without employment contracts the company must keep the climate challenging and invigorating and the rewards commensurate with the performance. Contracts in my opinion usually lose the men they are designed to hold. And keep those who have no other basis for staying.*

Robert Townsend, *Up The Organization*

The best strategy is to get a written job offer. Once you accept the offer by signing it, it becomes a valid, mutually binding, contract of employment. These days, most employers will send you a written job offer by mail. You will be given a few days to think about it and either reject it or sign it and return it to the employer.

Should you wish to add some clauses to an employment offer, ring the employer or go to see them personally and discuss the issue. Once you sign on the dotted line, you have to play by the rules you've agreed upon. Be persistent. Don't believe their usual story, such as 'We would have to retype the letter and wait for the General Manager to return from overseas/Dallas/Zanzibar/hospital to sign it'. If you can negotiate a better deal for yourself, go for it. Not many employers would withdraw a job offer if you make additional requests. They don't like guerrilla fighters, but they respect people who stand up for themselves.

So what should a properly written job offer contain?

- Your title and basic job duties
- Your place of work – department, location, branch or such like
- Working hours
- Salary, including overtime rates and bonuses or allowances
- The procedure for payment of salaries or wages
- The name and title of your immediate superior
- The day on which your employment commences
- The validity period of the offer (usually seven days)
- The name, address and telephone number of a person who can give you further information and clarify any points or answer any questions you may have.

If you have any questions or queries and there is no contact name on the offer, ring the person that interviewed you, or the person that signed the offer, and ask for clarification.

## Job descriptions

Job descriptions are a typical bureaucratic invention. In a modern working environment, where jobs are constantly changing in nature, job descriptions belong in the past.

*At best, a job description freezes the job as the writer understood it at a particular instant in the past. At worst, they're prepared by personnel people who can't write and don't understand the jobs. Then they are not only expensive to prepare and regularly revise, but they're important morale-sappers.*

Robert Townsend, *Up The Organization*

A job description in most cases serves as an additional guarantee to the employers that you will perform any task they ask you to, providing it's listed in the description. So, carefully analyse the document and question inappropriate tasks, or you may end up punching data into a computer or doing a foreman's job instead of the higher duties you believed were intended.

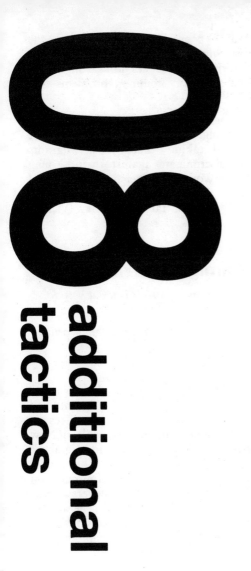

# 08

# additional
# tactics

**In this chapter you will learn:**
- about problems you may
  encounter in the job market
  because of discrimination
- how to look for another job
  while employed
- how to resign

This chapter is dedicated to people who are in some way disadvantaged in the interviewing process. The reasons for those disadvantages are different: the consequences differ from case to case, too. However, there are many common problems that those job seekers face.

The most interesting phenomenon among today's disadvantaged groups is the mutual blaming. Natives blame migrants for accepting lower wages and taking 'their' jobs. Migrants complain that employers discriminate against them. Young women blame older, married women for their inability to find jobs, while older women say the employers favour young girls because they do the same jobs for far less money. Victims against victims.

# Minorities and immigrants

*Experience is not what happens to you. It is what you do with what happens to you.*

Aldous Huxley, *Brave New World*

## The problem

Discrimination of some kind is a part of everyday life for many job hunters. The high unemployment rate for immigrants and minorities is a good indication that old habits and prejudices die hard. In the USA, for instance, about one-third of adults in New York, 44 per cent in Los Angeles and 70 per cent in Miami are foreign-born, according to the 1990 census. The report commissioned by the Australian Bureau of Immigration Research in November 1991 points out that 'employers appear to distinguish among immigrants from different generational and regional backgrounds in the employment decisions'. The report also found 'some evidence of disadvantage among first-generation young immigrants, particularly women'.

Some recruitment consultants openly and bluntly admit that immigrants, mainly from South-East Asia and India with the same qualifications as their English, American or Australian counterparts do not even have a look-in at the moment. The employers select people with whom they feel they could relate, and in many cases a candidate's résumé is dismissed because of the foreign name on the front page.

Some (or most?) managers do not have the tole... or broad views that are necessary to deal with em... different nationalities or backgrounds. Familiarity ... familiarity. The common excuse for such an attitude is th... famous phrase: 'local experience is necessary'.

Some employers realize that most immigrants have good skills and a high work ethic, and abuse that fact. Most immigrants are keen to work hard and are committed to their jobs, which leaves them open to exploitation. Their lack of knowledge of local conditions and various unwritten rules and employers' tricks and tactics makes them prepared to accept less attractive jobs and lower wages.

Before we take a look at the guerrilla tactics that could be used to overcome the problems mentioned above, let's define the criteria that make you a minority. At the first level, two things are obvious: the colour of your skin and your accent. Your background comes next, with details such as your nationality, age, the schools and universities you attended, your family history, etc. These are less important and can be concealed.

## Guerrilla tactics

So what could be done about all this? Unfortunately, it's very hard to change people's attitudes, so the only possible tactic is 'If you can't beat them, join them.' Sounds like a cliché, but here it is in a nutshell:

- Translate all your documents, diplomas, certificates and references to English and get them verified.
- Put in a lot of effort in the preparation of your résumé. If necessary, use outside help (and any help available). Make sure there are no spelling mistakes, no grammatical or syntax errors.
- Improve your English. The better your communication skills, the greater your chances for getting a job.
- If necessary, change your name. It may seem too drastic, but it will at least get you through the first round (when they knock out most résumés with foreign names on them) and let you have a fair go. I may be wrong, but I'm convinced that my Serbian name cost me at least a couple of attractive jobs in the past.
- Dress the way local people dress and behave the way they behave. From the moment you apply for the job, try to

...c habits and constraints. Always project
...and a 'globetrotter' image. You have been
...ve done it all. Many people never leave their
...nd admire (or at least envy) people who have
...d.

...ocal job market and the way recruiters and
...ink and work, analyse various companies, their
...nd philosophies. Read self-improvement books,
...gazines and newspaper advertisements and build
...a base for future job opportunities. Make a folder for
each ...f the big employers. That will help you determine their
way of thinking and recruiting.

# Women

## The problem

*Whatever women do they must do twice as well as men
to be thought half as good. Luckily this is not difficult.*

Charlotte Vitton in M. Rogers, *Contradictory
Quotations*

Global society is undergoing steady demographic change. The
biggest change has certainly been in the area of female
employment. More and more women are entering the work
force or returning to employment after the 'domestic' period of
starting a family and raising children.

Slowly, employers are changing their attitudes and prejudices
towards women. Equal opportunity policies are paving the way
to equality in treatment and pay between men and women.
However, women are still not equal with men when it comes to
employer's preferences and salary levels. Men are generally paid
more than the women who perform the same duties.

*Part of the problem could lie with women themselves,
due to their timidity and lack of energetic approach to
job hunting and later in the work environment.*

A recent study in the USA, which questioned 3,347
undergraduates at six of the country's most prestigious
universities, found that female students, on average, had lower
self-esteem and lower aspirations then their male counterparts.

## Re-entering the work force

If you belong to the growing group of women who are returning to part-time or full-time employment after a few years spent at home raising a family, you may find yourself disadvantaged in comparison with your competitors for the same jobs. Although you may not have relevant job experience, think about the skills and experience gained at home, in community service and in various club activities, that can be related to the requirements of the position you are applying for.

## Interviewers' fears about women

- They will get married and leave the company, get pregnant and leave, or follow their husbands and leave. In any case, they will leave soon and we'll have to invest time and money in recruiting another person.
- Women are too emotional, they can't control their emotions, they are often depressed and moody, and burst into tears under slightest pressure or stress.
- Women are not able to operate in a man's world, which is ruthless and competitive.
- Women cannot fit into male teams. They don't have the same values. They will add an element of sexuality in the team and spoil the male-to-male relationships.
- Women don't work as hard as men do. They are not dedicated to their jobs as men are. They view their jobs as places to meet a future husband.

If you are a woman, you have an additional task in front of you: to convince interviewers that any fears they have are without foundation, and that you can do your job as well as any man could, if not better.

# School leavers and graduates

*I have never let my schooling interfere with my education.*

Mark Twain

## The mistakes graduates make

For those of you who are looking for your first job in 'the real world', there are a few important points to remember. You will never have more control over the hiring process than in the beginning. That means you should not do what most graduates do:

- They send dozens of résumés to every possible employer they can think of and pray for some response. Due to the buyer's market they place themselves at the market's mercy.
- In selecting an employer they go for quick results and forget about long-term interests. They pay too much attention to starting salaries and benefits.
- They don't market and promote themselves properly, so some employers get them very cheap. Under the pretext of gaining experience, they perform work that would cost the employers much more had it been carried out by experienced professionals. Cheap labour? Maybe.

Young people, fresh out of college or university are the ones with greatest expectations and greatest potential, yet they are the ones that most companies tend to neglect. When such smart and ambitious employees (often thrown into an entry-level position and paid less than a cleaner) leave after a year or two for greener pastures, the employer is puzzled. For some strange reason they don't treat their employees as an investment. They don't train them properly or challenge them with projects that are beneficial to both employer and employee.

Some employers realize the pitfalls and expenses involved in losing talented young people and stretch them to their limits. These are the companies you should aim for. To get a job with them, you'll have to do your homework properly.

## Guerrilla tactics

With recent graduates, most companies look for signs of achievement, not only academic ones such as scholarships. They also want a business approach, self-discipline and election to leadership positions. You have to convince the employer that your academic success is the best indicator of your abilities and the sign of all great things you can do for them.

Here are some tips and strategies that every young achiever should consider:

- Select a company before it selects you. Be a chooser, not a beggar. Do your personal balance sheet properly and get to know yourself. Know what you want and devise a plan that will help you get it.

- Never stop learning. Be a student forever. When you finish school or graduate, the real learning process starts. Sounds strange, but it tells you something about the quality of today's education.
- Expect to succeed. Adopt a positive attitude. Despite all doom and gloom, feel confident in yourself, your abilities and your likelihood of success. Learn as much as possible, as soon as possible. Time is a precious asset because it's limited. We all have a certain number of years to live, so don't procrastinate and waste them.
- Take your career into your own hands. Be your own union. Nobody can protect your interests better than you can, yourself. Learn everything about your job as quickly as possible, then about the jobs your colleagues are doing, and about your boss's job, too. Do that, and you will be sitting in his chair sooner than you think.
- Use every opportunity to promote yourself. Be visible and make sure everybody knows when you do a good job. Market yourself aggressively. Attend seminars, conferences, product and trade shows, exhibitions, displays.
- Always keep an ace hidden up your sleeve. A cushion to fall on is a nice thing to have. Keep your options open. Don't overspecialize. Be universal and flexible. Cultivate your business relationships. If you ever lose your job, for any reason, there is a great chance that one of your business contacts may offer you another. Make sure you're ready when the opportunity knocks.

# People changing careers

*Try another profession. Any other.*

Head Instructor at John Murray Anderson Drama
School to Lucille Ball

The performance of an employee on the job is not a very accurate indicator of how he feels about his job, the company and his achievements. Some people do great jobs in the areas they are not really interested in. Their talent, discipline and hard work lead to good performance, but their real interests are somewhere else.

Most people who have changed their careers admit that there was a cost to achieving that change. Most of them had to face a considerable cut in income, at least initially. Some of them never caught up with their earnings in the old job, but they were much happier for doing things they really liked.

Some very illustrative cases were published in the book *Career Turnaround* by John Viney and Stephanie Jones. Make sure you read it before embarking on the career-changing path. As one interviewee said: 'You mustn't go to something new just because you think the grass is greener, and you mustn't run away from something, or you will be going from one unhappiness to another.'

If you think about career turnaround, you really have to analyse yourself thoroughly. You've got to know what your strengths and weaknesses are, and whether they match the goals you want to achieve. Whatever you do, think twice before you make such an important decision. Keep in mind that grass always looks greener on the other side of a fence. Sometimes a bird in the hand *is* worth two in the bush.

# Unemployed people

Being unemployed becomes reality for more and more people every day. Thousands of jobs are disappearing overnight as companies fight recessions. In their battle to become lean and mean, people from various backgrounds, different industries and with all sorts of qualifications find themselves on the streets. They are labourers, tradesmen, engineers, managers. Nobody's job is safe, fear and uncertainty become part of our lives.

*In comparison with people who are employed and want to change jobs, unemployed job hunters are definitely disadvantaged, due mostly to the prevalent employers' misconceptions.*

There is a view amongst employers that people who are employed would perform better in a job and some employment consultants claim that 80–90 per cent of the candidates taken by their clients were already in jobs. The fact that someone has been out of work for a long time can cast doubt in the mind of an employer about the overall quality of the applicant.

The additional difficulty that people with higher degrees face quite often is a definite reluctance among employers who are not engaged in research to employ them. They suspect that this type of employee will move on as soon as positions that suit their skills better become available. In addition, some managers feel uncomfortable working with people who are more qualified and possibly smarter than themselves. This could simply be called being over-qualified for the job.

## Self-esteem

The biggest problem for unemployed job seekers is the constant erosion of their self-esteem. They cannot escape the feeling of inferiority among people with regular employment, even though they may realize that their skills, knowledge and intelligence are far from inferior. The longer they are out of work, the worse it is for their morale. The first step towards consolidation is to boost your morale and self-esteem.

If you are selling yourself to a prospective employer you cannot allow your morale to drop, because there will be many other candidates who have confidence and self-esteem. Think positive, think optimism, growth and success.

In his excellent book *Maximise Your Mental Power*, Dr David Schwartz gives this advice: It isn't what one has that's important. Rather, it's how much one is planning to get that counts. The price tag the world puts on us is just about identical to the one we put on ourselves.

My advice to unemployed people is very simple:

> *Be a future-oriented person. Don't keep dwelling upon the past. The past won't get you employed.*

## Voluntary work

One of the options open to unemployed people is voluntary work. Should you opt for that approach, the first thing you should do is consider a few places where you want to work and offer your services to those employers. If successful, this will enable you to gain new skills and significantly increase your chances of getting a real job.

In addition to that, voluntary work will help you build your spirits up and maintain a positive mental attitude. It will keep you in contact with the working environment and serve as a credential, highly regarded by prospective employers. In competing with couch potatoes, who have been spending their time at home, watching midday soaps and waiting for employers to call them should the vacancy arise, you will be a clear winner.

If you are good at what you are doing, the whole situation will only be temporary. It is very likely that some sort of remuneration will be offered initially, such as free meals, bus or train fares, etc. As you keep doing a good job, your chances of getting a permanent job will multiply. A foot in the door can mean: 'The job is yours!'

For those of you who are unemployed and manage to get a job interview, the important point to remember is to explain your case to the interviewer. Don't hide anything or bend the facts. If your job was made redundant and you had to take the company's retrenchment package, that wasn't your fault and should have no impact on your ability to perform in the job for which you are interviewing.

# Interviewing while employed

*Do what you can, with what you can, where you are.*

Theodore Roosevelt

## The reason

So, day by day, your dissatisfaction grows. You are underpaid, or missed a promotion or a pay rise, your boss doesn't respect you, your co-workers are stabbing you in the back, your job is a bore, you disagree with the company's policies and rules. To cut a long story short: you want to get out.

It makes me very sad to see young, educated, hardworking and ambitious people unemployed or working for peanuts while other, less educated and less productive, people with almost no abilities or skills make a very good living while contributing nothing towards the common good. If you belong to the first group, read the rest of this chapter very carefully.

## Guerrilla tactics for underpaid professionals

*If you have invested large amounts of time and money to get a diploma or a degree and to advance to the professional level, you should be ferociously determined to get your investment back and with interest. From the employers and clients, of course.*

Lawyers and doctors have been practising this for years. Other professionals, such as engineers, architects or scientists, have even more right to do so, yet they are marginalized and sadly neglected. This is my advice to these job hunters:

- There is no union that protects your interests, therefore the onus is on you to protect what you have and acquire what you want. The end usually justifies the means.
- Practise professional courtesy. Make life easier for other members of your profession and for yourself. Never criticize or badmouth your colleagues. By helping make your profession recognized and appreciated you strengthen your own position tremendously.
- Project a busy and professional attitude. Let people (and employers) realize that your time is valuable and that your expectations are high. Be a no-nonsense person. Don't let them fool you or take you for granted.
- Learn as much as possible not only about your job, but about those of other people. That will give you an edge in dealings with them, broaden your horizons and prepare you for the top jobs.
- Be visible and market yourself. If your boss doesn't recognize your talents, be sure that his competitors will. If your boss is your obstacle to moving up, change your boss. Don't waste time.
- Whatever you do, believe in yourself. Remember the famous words: 'Day by day in every way I'm getting better and better' (Emile Coue, the author of *Self-mastery Through Autosuggestion*). The power of autosuggestion is enormous. Think positive, think big.
- Plan to win. The one element that stands out most clearly among high achievers is their strong belief in their success. They plan to win! From now on, I'm sure, you'll plan to win, too.

***If your boss doesn't recognize your talents, be sure that his competitors will.***

## Time constraints

Time is the biggest problem for job seekers who are still employed. It isn't easy to enquire about jobs and attend interviews while working from 8 to 5. But, there are some ways to overcome this obstacle. First of all, use your weekends for writing job applications, doing your research on employers and mastering your interviewing skills. Use your lunch hours for enquiries and other telephone contacts with employers.

If you have an appointment for an interview in the same city, take a day off if you can, preferably a paid day off. If you cannot, arrange an interview for a late afternoon, say 5 or 6 p.m. or Saturday morning. Many managers and recruiters work long hours, and will accommodate their plans to meet a promising candidate. If the position you are interested in is a long distance away, take two or more days off. Use your annual leave or unpaid days off. Specify the simple reason: Personal business.

Using your sick leave is another option. Most companies have a policy that for up to two days of sickness no medical certificate is necessary (in the UK you can self-certificate for up to five days). However, be careful when using sickness as an excuse, for there is always a chance that someone you know may see you in your grey suit, white shirt and a tie while you were supposed to be lying ill in bed.

## Feeling guilty

Some of you may feel guilty when looking for a job while still employed. I always felt the same. Then I realized that many other people were doing the same, even my boss and his manager. It is common practice in Western society. Employers have the right to terminate your employment at any time, if they can justify their decision. That justification could be poor performance (sacking) or redundancy (retrenchment).

They can prepare for that situation by training your replacement and by transferring some or all of your duties to your colleagues. You, an employee, have similar rights in protecting yourself from losing your job and in advancing your career. You also have the right to quit at any time and to prepare for the act of quitting through applying for other jobs and through interviewing with other employers.

## Keeping your mouth shut

There is one golden rule to remember, no matter what you do or what your job-hunting strategies are: *never* tell anybody that you are looking for a job. The only exceptions are the people that can help you in the process. Most people cannot keep a secret, and the last thing you want is for your employer to find out that you are looking for a better job. So don't trust anyone.

Never apply for a position if the advertisement gives only a post office box number. It could be a bogus advertisement and your application may end in the wrong hands or your name may appear on every mail-order list imaginable. Some less reputable mail-order companies do that. So do some employers, in order to 'probe' the market.

## Employment agencies

Even employment agencies should not be trusted. There is a chance that your résumé will finish on your employer's desk, through who knows what channels. Employment consultants are more loyal to employers, because it's the employers who pay their commissions. Candidates are a commodity, nothing more and nothing less.

In some cases, the existence of employment agencies can be justified. They bring employers and job hunters together. Most of the time, however, employers use personnel consultants to do their job for them, either because they have no time or expertise to select people or because they think that 'professional' head hunters would do a better job than they would. I consider that a big mistake. Not only does this cost them money, but they rely on others to select the right person for the job.

Alternative: write to potential employers directly. Do your own marketing. You'll create a much better impression if you directly approach the company you are interested in, for you display initiative and resilience. Skip the middle men. Employers pay them to find the candidates, so, naturally, they must get that money back from somebody. That somebody is you.

> *Don't quit until you've got that other job. Personnel departments, like banks, deal only with people who don't need them.*
>
> Robert Townsend, *Up the Organization*

# Leaving your employer

> *The son of a bitch (General MacArthur) isn't going to resign on me. I want him fired.*
>
> Harry S. Truman, attributed

When you resign, do it professionally, by handing a typewritten letter of resignation to your boss, his boss and the personnel manager. Be brief and concise. Don't go into too many details or try to explain why you're moving. State a simple reason: better opportunities elsewhere. Don't criticize, condemn or blame people or circumstances. Simply say you have enjoyed working for them, learned a lot from capable people you had the privilege to work with (don't mention idiots, incompetents or bastards). Only nice things should be found in your resignation letter. Honesty may make you feel good for a moment, but would prove devastating later, when you need a reference.

Some companies have a policy of using so-called 'exit interviews'. Every employee who resigns and leaves 'for greener pastures' goes for a 'chat' with his or her manager and/or one of the 'personnel people', who try to establish where they have failed in their efforts to motivate you and make you happy working for them.

Should you find yourself in such an interview, make sure you don't say anything you may regret later. Personnel people have very good memories. That's part of their job; to remember who did what, who said what and who thinks what. They are the intelligence service within a company. They use subtle methods, or at least don't use open intimidation. But rest assured that black books are still in use, along with 'in' and 'out' lists, where a person's fate is determined with a stroke of a pen.

Another important point to be considered is references. Unloading your frustration and telling your employer what you really think of them is not good policy in the exit interview; it may make you feel good for a while, but you'll pay for it later, when you need a reference. When you leave, part on friendly terms. Don't burn your bridges behind you.

The best (or least damaging) reasons for leaving you can use include:

- I was offered a more senior position with higher salary and the opportunity for rapid career growth.
- Although I enjoyed my stay here, I decided to move due to family reasons.
- I have enjoyed working here, but I felt I needed more experience in _____ (*the area in which you couldn't develop your skills*), so I decided to search for a position where I could develop those skills.

- While I was specializing in _____, I felt I was lacking broader experience in various aspects of_____ (*accounting, engineering, marketing, etc.*).
- I have decided to start my own business. The experience gained with this company will be very beneficial in my future efforts.

Some of the worst (make sure you don't even remotely imply them) reasons for leaving (although, in most cases, these will be the real causes of discontent) include:

- My boss didn't appreciate my efforts and didn't respect me. He was an idiot and didn't know how to treat people.
- This company doesn't value its employees. I feel like a number. There is no genuine concern for employees and no open communication between workers and management.
- This is a dead-end job. It's unchallenging and boring and I couldn't wait to get out.
- This position is way below my qualifications and expertise. My knowledge and talents were not used, so I wanted to get out at the first opportunity.
- I considered this position only as an interim measure, until I find something that really interests me and that fits my career plans. I have found such a position, so I would like to terminate my employment with your company.

# 09

## final advice

Job hunting is a game. Sometimes you win, sometimes you lose. It is a different game than, say, the Olympic Games, where the emphasis is on participating: in job hunting, you should play to win. Winning is the most important thing in life and nothing else can be compared with the feeling of winning.

On the other hand, losing is not necessarily bad. It should teach you how to improve your performance and win more often. Smart people learn from their mistakes, analyse them and never repeat the same mistake twice. The top performers learn from other people's mistakes. That should be your goal, too.

> *Don't despair if your first interviews turn out to be failures. Keep trying.*

People say: 'Practice makes perfect'. I would add to that 'Perfect practice makes perfect'. The best way to practise is to apply for some jobs you don't really want or need, just to get as much experience in interviewing as possible. When the big opportunity comes up you'll be ready to use that experience. That will give you a big advantage over your competitors. They will lack practice and knowledge of the interviewing process. They will be uneasy, nervous and will sell their abilities short. You, on the other hand, will be 'battle-hardened'. You will recognize questions, fears, tricks and traps and use advanced tactics, proven in your previous interviews.

To get the job you want and to steer your career in the right direction, you must take one step at a time, but each step should lead you to your final goal: success. Success is a relative word, its meaning varies with different people. But to me there is only one definition of real success: to be able to spend your life the way *you* want!

There are two possible paths for career advancement. In the first, you jump around from company to company. If you learn quickly, know how to make friends, handle people and lever your skills and knowledge into a better position, this path is for you. You have to keep your eyes and ears open, keep in touch with people, regularly refresh your knowledge, upgrade your existing skills and acquire new ones.

The alternative approach is to grow within one company. Big players are particularly suitable for this method. In some cases just by staying with the employer long enough you can get to the top. This takes patience and persistence. You have to master corporate games and office politics. This is probably the more difficult path, especially in today's business climate.

I consider career leapfrogging the quickest way to get to the top. Days of loyalty to one employer, one idea or one product are gone and forgotten. Your employer is not loyal to you: you are on a few weeks' notice. That's all his loyalty. So why should you be loyal to your employer?

In his excellent book *Confessions of an S.O.B.*, Al Neuhart gives this advice: 'Be your own pitchman. Sell yourself. Attention does not come quickly to the humble.' Remember this, you'll need it.

*This is all that the job interview is: a sales presentation. It is the only sales presentation where the product sells itself. That product is you.*

## At the end

*Advice is judged by results, not by intentions.*
Cicero, *Ad Atticum IX*

The interviewing tactics you've learned in this book should prove useful in your current and future job hunting endeavours. However, the final results will depend not only on your skill but also on the skills of the people interviewing you. Some amateurish interviewers will be steamrollered by your use of your advanced strategies. Some experienced professionals, on the other hand, will be able to recognize you as a 'professional interviewee' and will put more effort into evaluating you.

Some of them will read this book, I guess, and come up with countermeasures for neutralizing your efforts. But don't despair. Not all of them are so professional and astute to figure you out.

Looking for a job and employment interviewing is one of the loneliest, the most difficult and the most frustrating businesses in the world. Many times you'll feel down and out, you'll question your abilities, lose your self-confidence, feel discouraged and disillusioned. To achieve your goal you'll have to fight all those negative thoughts and feelings. I cannot stress enough how important it is to maintain a positive attitude. If you don't believe in yourself, nobody will. Apart from believing in your own abilities, you'll need stamina, perseverance and hard work. And a bit of luck, of course.

*I'm a great believer in luck, and
the harder I work, the luckier I get.*
Stephen Leacock, Canadian Humorist

So, at the end of our job hunting and interviewing journey, I hope I have given you a better idea of how recruiters think and what they want to hear at a job interview. The last thing I can do for you is wish you all the best in your current and future efforts in finding the 'top job' you deserve.

# index